Don't Talk
Don't Trust
Don't Feel

Our Family Secrets

Robert A. Becker, Ph.D.

Health Communications, Inc.
Deerfield Beach, Florida

Library of Congress Cataloging-in-Publication Data

Becker, Robert A.
    Don't talk, don't trust, don't feel : our family secrets / by Robert A. Becker.
    p. cm.
    ISBN 1-55874-127-5
    1. Problem families — Psychological aspects. 2. Adult children of dys-
funtional families — Psychology. 3. Communication in the family.
I. Title
HV697.B43   1991
158'.24 — dc20   90-46470
                                                                                        CIP

© 1991 Robert A. Becker
ISBN 1-55874-127-5

Publisher: Health Communications, Inc.
              3201 S.W. 15th Street
              Deerfield Beach, Florida 33442

Dedication

To my wife Deborah.

Acknowledgments

There are several people who shared their thoughts and ideas for this book. And I shall acknowledge them in a moment. Yet the continuing source of information my patients have provided over the years has fueled the development and theories I have assembled. To them I am grateful for their openness and trust.

I want to thank Claudia Black, whose pioneering work and ideas with ACoAs acted as a springboard for this book.

Two close personal friends listened many a night to my ravings as the book evolved: Carla Wills-Brandon and Joy Miller.

As usual, my kids regularly play a role in my books. For without them, there might never be a book. To David, Jason, Robert, Patrick, Matthew, and Gary — thanks, guys.

As always, I am grateful to my wife Deborah. There are so many things I could acknowledge her for, but the main one is just putting up with me through this project. As readers of my first book know, that book was completed on my honeymoon. This one was concluded on our family vacation. Her endearing comment about this, "I wouldn't know what to do on a trip if you weren't writing — but I'm quickly learning."

Contents

Introduction

Family Secrets Of Adult Children

In recent times, the notion of "adult child" has been synonymous with those people who grew up in alcoholic families. These were families that not only had significant traumas and problems, but that, as a result of their characteristics, had secrets: things about the family not discussed in public (don't talk); rules that demanded feelings be silent (don't feel); and the basic underlying theme that "you can't trust anyone" (don't trust). As a result, the secrets acted to cement the family members in dysfunctional ideas, attitudes and behaviors. In particular, the children experienced many distortions of reality. These may have included:

- Learning not to believe what grown-ups said due to their unreliability.
- Thinking that the feelings they had were bad and should not be expressed.
- Never feeling they had anything important to share.
- Being expected to take on adult responsibilities and roles, missing their own childhood experiences.

Undoubtedly there are others, but these secrets were enough to affect the child in such a way that he was prepared for a life of despair, unhappiness and emotional unfulfillment. Without question, the alcoholic family's dysfunction spawned many adult children, and the "family secrets," with all their ramifications, moved on to the next generation, as these adults then shared what they had learned in their families.

For years as I worked with adult children from alcoholic families, I discovered how extremely similar their interpersonal problems were to those of other adults who too had experienced dysfunctions in their families. Adults whose parents divorced or separated, had a physical or mental illness, or experienced emotional and physical abuse presented virtually the same childhood traumas and family secrets as their alcoholic counterparts.

Although all children from dysfunctional families are not affected in the same manner and their level of resilience to the conditions is controlled by many variables, adults from these environments had the most difficulty with self-concept, feelings of competency and interpersonal relationship skills. The family secrets or rules so often were the very same ones seen in the alcoholic family. The result: An "adult child" population that includes many more persons than just those of alcoholic families.

The journey through this book is for those of us who lived with these family secrets and became adult children. The goal of this book is to help us discover and identify why we've spent so much energy in maintaining poor marriages and relationships, stayed at jobs which never fulfilled any of our needs and, most importantly, never been able to feel good about ourselves and our accomplishments.

In order to do this, we must look carefully at our family of origin and the issues surrounding that family's dynamics. Understanding basic human behavior and the learning that occurs through our reward and punishment system are next. Finally, we must find solutions to help us change years of indoctrination and reinforcement, if any meaningful attempt at recovery is to happen. The impact on a child, learning and living with the family secrets of not talking, trusting or feeling, is so profound that we must find ways to reverse those catastrophic instructions.

By looking at how such things as bonding, enmeshment and boundaries developed, we can create a treatment plan to set the road for our recovery. So often, people come to our offices seeking our help, as professionals, presenting what seems to be "extraordinary circumstances." That is, their situations are often traumatic or even catastrophic. The role they are in has been played for years, not only by them, but by those who originated it generations before. Yet, as adult children, they are just attempting to survive one more life situation.

As therapists we often react to their situations by prescribing "extraordinary solutions" to their problems. Meanwhile the dysfunctional model they have always been a part of now continues with their therapy. Life has always been a matter of survival, not problem- or task-solving, and as therapists we've just given them one more way to survive — in lieu of solving the problem.

Treating their symptoms is easier. Often the symptoms are misdiagnosed as the problem. They become enmeshed in our needs as professionals to "fix or rescue" them. Instead, we should be helping them make a careful inspection of how their family system operated and what the family secrets were so they may begin healing, finding themselves and growing, ultimately moving through the maze of recovery.

Not too long ago, my seven-year-old Matthew was learning the basics of arithmetic, adding and subtracting. I recall explaining one night to him why 1 + 1 = 2. And why it didn't equal three or four or whatever. Being the good compliant parent I am and not wanting to rock the foundations of elementary education (especially those of Catholic school, where after the second time you got your name on the board, you might lose your lunch privileges), I began to develop the understanding needed to see why *learning reversal* was so difficult.

Everybody and everything in the system of a child supported this idea that 1 + 1 = 2. To pretend that it might be something else (1 + 1 = 3) would be sheer mutiny, punishable by severe measures. More than likely for Matthew, if he were to deviate from the norm and begin some new creative mathematics, certainly lunch and playground privileges would cease.

This analogy of one of life's small experiences only echoes the significant relevance of how difficult and resistant it is to change belief and attitude systems, as well as the roles we've played for so long. This book will take you through a step-by-

step analysis of your family of origin and the resulting effects
on its members. The therapeutic value of this will help significantly in defining roles, identifying boundaries and noting
where personal growth stopped and dysfunction began. Then
we'll see how dysfunction maintains itself and spawns in each
new generation, unless intervention occurs. I'll describe methods that will help you disassociate from the enmeshment, as
well as reestablish boundaries.

No family-of-origin book would be complete, I feel, unless
it looked closely at how the spirit of our child got trapped
and how as our body grew into an adult, our emotional self
remained dormant. An adult who has lost his childhood cannot function as an emotionally mature individual. So discovering ways to let this child come out from within is another
point to be addressed here.

Not talking, feeling and trusting are the family secrets guiding and controlling the family and its members. These secrets
require us to examine the parenting we received, for this
parenting set the stage for the development of our emotional
value system. A child exposed to constant belittling will only
mature into an adult who feels inadequate and worthless. The
secrets of the dysfunctional family impact on us in so many
ways that, until we understand the emotional part they play,
we cannot begin to untangle the disorder of co-dependency.

Not dealing with the trauma of a dysfunctional family only
allows the resulting stress to continue, affecting not only us,
but those we care about. Recapturing what was lost in our
childhoods is impossible, but having someone teach us how
to parent and be good to ourselves *is* possible. This book will
unlock those issues which have kept us hostage to so much
pain and misery, and show us how to begin the process of
recovery and self-acceptance.

Family secrets for the adult child — don't talk, don't trust,
don't feel — lay the basic framework for our dysfunction. They
develop the fabric which weaves us into over-responsive, over-
sensitive, vulnerable adults. This manifests itself in our unsatisfying relationships, career selections and chronic emo-

tional instability. We have needs that are never met, goals we cannot attain and we discount our successes.

Not talking, trusting and feeling is too high a price to pay for a dysfunctional emotional security system. Think of how paradoxical that notion is. Why would anyone want a dysfunctional anything, let alone a security system? Imagine the problems created by dysfunctional burglar and fire alarms. Or dysfunctional pregnancy tests or whatever.

That which acts to identify, warn and engage our resources to deal with whatever life puts before us, must be in proper order. Under the best of circumstances, it seems difficult to have it functioning that way at all times. But our emotional security system, which monitors those things for us, cannot afford to be dysfunctional. If it is, we must make every effort to remedy the inadequacies and set into place those things which will maintain its proper functioning. Talking, trusting and feeling are all normal elements which keep our spirits and souls on track.

In the past decade much has been written about the adult child of alcoholics (ACoA). Long-overdue attention, recognition and help have resulted. The recovery process has been broadened by the co-dependent movement. Yet there remains a significantly larger population of people who worry obsessively, feel inadequate about themselves, are perfectionistic, try to please everyone, are self-victimizing and just seem to find misery everywhere.

In my first book, *Addicted To Misery: The Other Side Of Co-dependency,* I referred to these people as misery addicts. If we look at their families of origin, we notice that they may not have lived with Ward and June Cleaver (Wally's and Beaver's parents; funny, I don't recall ever meeting anyone who did), but they didn't live with Mommie Dearest either. Their exposure to extreme family dysfunction may have been less than that of a raging, violent alcoholic family. Yet their emotionless, demanding, rigid, perfectionistic and controlling families created the right mix to instill the unhappiness they came to know. While becoming enmeshed in their family's dynamics, their childhoods froze. The result was learning to reenact those very roles and beliefs so clearly portrayed in the family.

Learning to talk about needs, discovering feelings and beginning to trust your own judgment is the mission of this book. At the end of each chapter is a section entitled *Laboratory Experiments*. The exercises give you an opportunity to evaluate yourself in relation to the material presented and help you work through the necessary processes of healing. Our family secrets which have controlled us for so long need to be destroyed. Solutions to stopping the dysfunction, ending the misery and beginning recovery are the goals to be achieved.

Good Luck And God Bless!

Don't Talk, Don't Trust, Don't Feel

Don't Talk:
>to him, he's busy
>>he has a hangover
>>he's angry
>
>to her, she's preoccupied with him
>>she's frightened for her safety, her sanity
>>she's angry
>
>to strangers, they don't understand that he loves her
>>or he wouldn't hit her
>>that he loves us, so he has to leave
>>that she loves him and us, so she can't cope
>
>to friends, they don't understand that the smiling
>>thoughtful man is the same one who beats his wife
>>the same one who abandons his family
>>the same one who calls me stupid
>
>to God,
>>He doesn't answer

Don't Trust:
>that he will stay this time
>that he won't spend all our money on pinochle,
>>booze, friends and strangers at the bar
>that he will keep his promises to take us
>>to the circus, the movies, the park
>that he will remove his hands from Mom's screaming
>>neck because he hears our sobbing pleas
>that God will answer my prayers
>>to bring him back
>>to send him away
>>to take my pain

Don't Feel:
    the pain of loss each time he walks out of the door
    the ache of enmeshed hate/love/hate
    the anger of a child fighting for food, for shelter, for warmth
    the loss of innocence when a 10-year-old child
        pulls a butcher knife from her mother's shaking hand
    the despair of knowing God doesn't answer my pleas
        to bring him back
        to send him away
        to take my pain

Connie Lakey, 1989

One

The Adult Child

Over the past decade, this phenomenon of the adult child has been defined, written about in books, discussed on radio and television talk shows, and been the topic of conferences and workshops people have attended to discover more about themselves.

The original term "adult child" was used in connection with adults who grew up in alcoholic families as children. This particular set of adults seemed to share many of the same emotional and social characteristics which often resulted in common problems for them. Unsatisfying relationships, unrewarding jobs and general personal despair seemed to manifest itself everywhere for the adult child. Intuitively, these adults were insecure, untrusting, emotionally repressed, angry and extremely controlling people.

Claudia Black in her book *It Will Never Happen To Me* outlined the cardinal rules of these families: Don't Talk, Don't Trust,

Don't Feel. She is credited with identifying these family laws and how they affected the members of the alcoholic family. As a result, these families propelled their children into adulthood, living life from an emotional point of view, always feeling victimized or chronically needing to take care of everyone.

The Caretaker

The caretaker adult child is seen as being obsessed with taking care of everyone else's needs and wants, while ignoring his or her own. It appears that self-esteem and identity can be achieved only through others. Psychologists explain that people who have an "external locus of control" seek out self-satisfaction almost exclusively from persons and things external to themselves. The caretaker adult child follows this design. She might say, "I'll be happy only if I can make you happy." Or, "I never feel satisfied unless I can make everyone else feel satisfied first."

It appears that this orientation comes from the anger adult children had for themselves, which resulted from the many failures and inadequacies they felt in meeting and satisfying everyone's needs in their families.

In their quest to please everyone, to reduce or stop the insanity of their alcoholic family, they only felt more and more failure with each unsuccessful attempt. Yet they remained convinced that normality would return if they "just did things right" or "made everyone feel better."

The Victim

The adult child victim plays out his anger from a dysfunctional childhood by reenacting many of the violent, hostile and hostage-taking scenes with the people he interacts with.

Blaming and making excuses for all the problems maintains this adult child's chronic misery with life. These adult children say, "My life wouldn't be such a mess if it weren't for . . . ," setting the blame outside of themselves. These people often believe everything that goes wrong in their lives is because . . . "it's them."

These two roles are clearly seen in most adult children of alcoholic parents. However, as we look at the notion of adult children in more generic ways, that is, beyond the influence of the alcoholic family, we begin to see that many other families are breeding grounds for the development of adult children. In fact, for so many of us, experiences of dysfunction or brokenness in our families was commonplace.

The family laws described by Claudia Black could be seen in many families. Often children are instructed not to talk about Mother's and Father's constant arguing, leaving the child confused and frightened about "What will happen next?" Both the children and adults in the divorcing home became mistrustful of each other and themselves. In the emotionally abusive family, members learned to repress or "stuff" their own feelings, so as not to create more conflict.

The result has spawned an entire group of adults suffering from a variety of emotional, social and interpersonal issues: the new adult child. I've created a definition that describes what this adult child may be:

Adult Child: *noun,* A term used to describe an adult person who has experienced some break in the normal developmental sequence as a child, such that the needed childhood experiences were delayed, rearranged or skipped altogether. In almost all cases, this resulted in the child growing into adulthood with an inadequate experience base to cope with personal and emotionally intimate situations. He often feels "childlike" or unequipped to deal with things as an "adult."

Developmental psychologists note that ordinal progress through a child's developmental stages is important for a healthy adulthood. This sequence serves to prepare the child for his adolescent life and then adulthood. Simply put, if the developmental sequence a child follows is altered, delayed or skipped, there will be some resulting dysfunction. The level and degree of this dysfunction will depend on the severity of the stage disrupted.

It then begins to make sense that our family of origin plays a significant part in how we come to be as functioning adults.

Our basic emotional security system, that which serves to protect and help us through the myriad of life's problems, is (at best) no better than what we experienced in our families as children.

It seems that those adults who emerged from rather dysfunctional families and appear to have adequate emotional defenses, were ones who were able to "debrief" or talk about the traumas as they occurred. This could have been accomplished with brothers, sisters or just a friend. This process is very similar to any other debriefing experiences people have following other traumas.

Talking about the experience appears to lessen the long-term effect and improve ongoing resilience. I will go into this process of debriefing in greater detail later. Yet, for many of us, little or no debriefing occurred. We were forced to hold onto the ideas, attitudes and beliefs our families taught us, leaving us, even as children, with adult responsibilities, distortions of realities, unhealthy boundaries and most painfully, shattered spirits.

The New Adult Child

The original concept of adult child evolved from those who grew up in alcoholic families. The notion that children were to be "seen and not heard" was often the mode of family operations. Those kids routinely had catastrophic experiences and the calm periods between traumas only begat hypervigilance and free-floating anxiety. The child's ability to trust those adults around him didn't exist; the main feeling experienced was anger. Generally everyone was angry with everyone. All the other feelings were ignored or squashed as soon as they surfaced.

The alcoholic family developed a unique sense of balance that supported this dysfunction and wouldn't tolerate anyone attempting to alter that state. Virginia Satir is credited with looking at family systems and defining how this balance existed and the manner in which members of the family were cast into one of several roles.

This delicate balance became the fabric which kept the family locked into dysfunction and sickness. The family system actually supported unhealthy attitudes and behaviors, and attacked any attempt to alter the balance.

Laura's Story

As an example, Laura lived in an alcoholic family. Physical abuse was absent, but emotional distress was constant. At an early age Laura's mother became psychotic and was hospitalized. Up until that time, she had been her father's favorite child: best in school, most cooperative and social, a model child. She remembers having her 10th birthday and, the next day, Mother going to the hospital. From that time on, she recalls becoming the "scapegoat" for the family.

Her alcoholic father turned toward her to care for the six smaller children and, in his drunken stupor, would tell Laura how inadequate she was. This "inadequate scapegoat" role had been her mother's for many years. But since Mother had become ill, this scapegoat role (someone to blame things on) was up for grabs.

Someone had to assume it and in the ensuing months, she remembered how crazy things seemed until she settled into this role. Mother's illness disturbed the delicate balance of the family, which required the casting of someone into her role.

Funny, Laura noted, once she became enmeshed in Mother's old role, life returned to "normal," as long as she played the part. The balance of the family returned, and the members were once again able to assume their own roles.

However, as I noted, many others of us had dysfunction in our families, but not that of the alcoholic family. Divorce, death, physical or mental illness are just a few dysfunctions which set the stage for children to experience significant voids or gaps, resulting in developmental impairments. These conditions, depending on their severity and length, affect the emerging adult in many of the same ways, as they affect children from alcoholic families.

These families, too, create unique roles for each member to foster and maintain during the dysfunctional period. Again, the balance is critical to the system's operation. The bottom line is that we have a newly defined adult child population with many of the same characteristics as their alcoholic adult child counterparts, but without the alcoholic family being present.

Family dysfunctions come in many varieties. Rigid, idealistic, emotionally controlled and perfectionistic families are the breeding ground for many of our new adult children.

Barbara's Story

Barbara grew up in such a family. She was the youngest of three children and her brothers were the "apple of Mother's eye." She never felt anything she did was good enough. She attended a strict religious school where guilt, shame and self-sacrifice were the primary lessons she recalled. These ideals were reinforced at home, creating an environment that prepared her for a life of anger, resentment, guilt and selfishness.

She found herself in three empty, abusive and repressive marriages, and projected her intense self-anger toward her children most of their lives. The result was children who became enmeshed in her own misery and self-disappointments.

Her family of origin set into play the roles and rules for Barbara's life. This created an emotional balance such that, if she were to deviate from its familiarity, it would make her so uncomfortable that she would quickly find a way to return to her dysfunctional ways. She told me about dating men who treated her in an egalitarian manner. She would either feel threatened by her lack of self-confidence, or have an extreme need to dominate the relationship to avoid feeling controlled. In many cases, these behaviors acted to sabotage the relationship. For Barbara, happiness and self-actualization never had a chance.

From early on in her family, those necessary elements which instill self-confidence, competence and esteem were absent. The developmental impairment which occurred resulted in an adult whose childhood prepared her for chronic dissatisfaction, unhappiness and misery.

Bonding, Enmeshment And Boundaries: Preparing Us For The Journey

As we can see, the characteristics and roles of the models in our family of origin often become bonded to us like wallpaper to a wall. Then we begin acting out of their dysfunctions. This is enmeshment: getting caught up in someone else's dysfunction. Interestingly, acting out the dysfunction seems greater if the dysfunction was done covertly (in a hidden or disguised way) rather than overtly (openly and publicly).

Finally, the family shows us boundaries and teaches us how to set limits. Things like what is allowable and what is not. How far we can go without consequences and what to expect. When it is safe to trust and when it is not. Anything that shows us an area to operate within, or how to make decisions about ourselves, deals with the ideas of boundaries and limits.

If the family's boundaries are ever-changing or not present at all, the result is confusion, distrust, feelings of aimlessness and worry. Learning to set healthy limits in these conditions is impossible.

Bill's Story

As an example, Bill had an extremely poor self-image and lacked confidence. He was a successful accountant with all the amenities of life, including a wonderful family. However, nothing ever seemed right or good enough for him. His ideas of success and self-satisfaction were unrealistic. When I questioned him about these negative feelings in our first interview, I asked which of his parents did he think he might be most like. He responded by saying that his father struggled with these very same feelings.

Father was successful but lacking in self-confidence or satisfaction. It was interesting, however, that he never observed his father showing these negative feelings overtly. But he said that his dad never thought of himself in positive ways:

"It wasn't what Dad said, but you could just tell he was never happy with his accomplishments," he recalled. "It was like I didn't know about his self-dissatisfactions, but I really did . . . we all really did . . . it was confusing."

Bill shared how his father had been abandoned as a small boy by his parents and then raised by an abusive alcoholic aunt and uncle. Then the picture began to fit. His father's feelings of inadequacy had a defined origin, yet he had never been able to deal with them. Father's inadequacies were transmitted covertly and Bill, being bonded to Dad, became enmeshed in his father's feelings of inadequacy.

His inability to stop those unhappy self-feelings became a problem Bill found impossible to resolve. This was because he was trying to fix a problem of his *father's*, not his own. Bill had only taken on the feelings, not actually done anything that compensated for having them. Bill's continuation of putting himself down as an adult was just a continuation of the same inappropriate behavior he had received as a boy.

The same thing happened to his father. His father grew up in an environment where the boundaries changed dramatically and his ability to learn how to set limits about such things as self-concept didn't develop. These same dysfunctional ideas became part of Bill's childhood, creating an adult with all the feelings of inadequacy his male role model, his dad, had presented. With no intervention, the cycle continued unbroken.

The child who bonds to a parent with an interpersonal dysfunction, such as feelings of inadequacy, incompetency or worthlessness (and those postures are presented to the child in very covert ways), becomes a child who is incapable of talking about himself (don't talk), trusting himself (don't trust) or expressing feelings (don't feel), or others.

Laboratory Experiments

1. Caretaking and victimizing are significant roles in dysfunctional families which start us on the road to becoming adult children. On a sheet of paper or the one provided here, draw a line down the middle and label one side "caretaker" and the other "victim." Now write the names of each family member that you remember playing those roles. Under that, list the caretaking behaviors you recall and how the victims described *their* victimization. As an example, caretaker behavior includes: attending to everyone else's needs and never to *their* own. Victims complain about always being used. Try to recollect as many as you can.

_____

_____

_____

_____

_____

_____

_____

_____

_____

_____

_____

_____

_____

_____

2. We talked about the importance of developmental stages for children and noted that if the child's environment resulted in his experiencing a delay, skip or rearrangement of these stages, this would begin the "adult child" cycle. Write out what impairments may have occurred for you as a child. An example would be having to be emotionally available for your dysfunctional parent, i.e., parenting the parent. List all the non-child roles and behaviors you had to perform in picking up the slack for your sick parent(s).

3. Remembering the family secrets of don't talk, don't trust, and don't feel, write out each one. Next to them, identify how your family defined which boundaries existed for these secrets. As an example:

Don't talk — our family made it clear that its business was private and never to be spoken in public. Things like money, sex, religion or politics were "off limits." The boundaries were precisely determined and consequences were present.

Caretaker

_____
_____
_____
_____
_____
_____
_____
_____
_____
_____
_____

Victim

_____
_____
_____
_____
_____
_____
_____
_____
_____
_____

Caretaking Behaviors

_____
_____
_____
_____
_____
_____
_____
_____
_____
_____
_____
_____

Describe Victimization

_____
_____
_____
_____
_____
_____
_____
_____
_____
_____
_____

TWO

My Family
Of Origin

Origin: *noun,* 1. thing from which anything comes:
sources, beginning. 2. parentage, ancestry, birth.

Family Of Origin: A Multigenerational Affair

Family of origin is really a simple concept to understand. It
is the people we grew up with in our family: mother, father,
brothers, sisters, grandparents, aunts, uncles or any other people whom we interacted with in our home on a regular basis.

We can look at family of origin on two levels. First, those
who were part of our daily family life are our primary family
of origin. Secondly, those relatives who impacted upon our
primary family of origin members, in their lives, became our
secondary family of origin.

Looking at how these two groups affected us, forms the foundation of family of origin work. By gathering the data these two groups present to us, we begin to assess the multi-generational effects family of origin had on each of us. This is not complicated. Just as positive traits and postures get passed on from generation to generation, so do negative or dysfunctional ones.

Some examples: Attending school, needing to study, making good grades and graduating are important concepts to many parents for their children. If these attitudes are part of the parents' belief and value system, this posture is transmitted by the parents. It may then become the family of origin trait to promote academic importance which would be considered a positive trait or posture. In the same manner, racial or religious prejudices travel from one generation to the next. The role models of the family continue to influence the children in representing the beliefs, attitudes and feelings to be followed. In the case of prejudices, this family of origin trait may begin by setting the first family secret to be observed in the home . . . don't trust. Once the trait is set by the family, each generation finds it more difficult to let it go or break away from the "family tradition." If it has become a family secret, it makes it even more difficult because the rules of the family generally prevent discussing the secret outside of the family (don't talk).

Many of our family traditions result from this multigenerational family of origin model. Things like family pride, leadership and motivation are all examples of things which may become multigenerational family of origin issues that get passed on. Probably one of the most written about and publicly exposed families where these specific traits were the mainstay of daily life are the Kennedys. Generational values such as the need to be leaders, striving for excellence and success and always being proud of your family are hallmarks in their family passed down through every generation.

Consider now the alcoholic family. Traits and attitudes such as mistrust, inadequacy, blaming and fear of failure become dominant. Given the nature of the family's secrets, these postures are maintained in such a way that, with each generational passing, they become more difficult to break. If unaddressed, their multigenerational effects render the recipients helpless from their dysfunctional by-products. These are the dynamics that get passed on. Mistrust begets mistrust, inadequacy begets inadequacy and so on with every negative feature. For example, adults who are angry, mistrusting and overachieving so often pass these postures on to their children. They, in turn, experience these values and grow into adulthood with the same beliefs, ready to continue the pattern with their own children. *Voila!* This is a multigenerational family of origin dysfunction.

At first glance it would appear that as we discover what effects our family of origin had on our emotional development, we would have reason enough to blame them for our pain and suffering. We must instead start by identifying what we saw what we didn't see but felt or somehow knew; what the personalities, goals, attitudes, feelings and postures were. This will set us on the road to understanding — not blaming — how things impacted us. I'm going to spend more time on this blaming issue later, but for now it's best to know our primary mission is that of understanding. Getting emotionally bogged down with blaming will only continue the same dysfunctional process which has operated for years maintaining our adult child characteristics.

Along my path of life, I encountered several multigenerational postures. Cynicism and mistrust had deep roots on my father's side of the family. On the surface, you would hear things like, "You can't trust them. All they want to do is take you for everything you have." Or, "I wouldn't trust that so-and-so with anything." The cynical and untrusting posture was very overt, yet the real covert postures being presented were their feelings of insecurity and lack of self-confidence and assurance. The dysfunctional pieces passed on became the covert ones.

My sister became enmeshed in my father's feelings of inadequacy, poor self-image and lack of self-confidence. Early on in school she struggled, not because of an intellectual deficit, but from those characteristics she became enmeshed in from my father. To this day, many of those feelings continue to affect her self-concept.

In so many of my clients' lives, this concept of becoming enmeshed in the covert dysfunctional attitudes and postures was regularly seen. The hidden messages, unspoken words and contradicting behaviors of the primary caregivers in our families were key elements in bonding us to them and their characteristics. Willing to do virtually anything as children, we followed and learned to gain approval, acceptance and most importantly, love.

Techniques To Examine Family Of Origin

Virginia Satir pioneered the early family of origin and system work. She described roles each member of the family took on like actors in a play. The family's dysfunction required a balance to maintain itself and each member would get cast into a role and be required to play it. It was here that each person would learn what was expected of her, along with what would happen if someone deviated from her role. In order to maintain the balance in a dysfunctional family, "survival roles" are created as a means of adjusting. The members then carry on with these roles as a way of relating to others. Often they maintain them for life, taking the dysfunction from one family to the next. Let's look at each survival role, which we have adapted from Sharon Wegscheider Cruse's Family Roles.

Chief Enabler:

Assumes primary responsibility for sheltering the dysfunctional family person from harmful consequences of behavior. This person uses defenses as a way to cover up true feelings and lives in the trap of self-delusion.

**CHIEF ENABLER
SPOUSE, PARENT, FRIEND, CO-WORKER**

wall of defenses

powerlessness

haughty

feelings

hurt

seriousness

anger   fear

self-pity

guilt   pain

self-blending

manipulation

super responsibility

The wall of defenses compulsively covers up the true feelings and the enabler lives in the trap of self-delusion.

FIGURE A

Family Hero:

Assumes responsibility for being the family's self-worth and family counselor. Internal emotions are in direct conflict with external behaviors.

FAMILY HERO

wall of defenses

success

works hard for approval

feelings

loneliness   hurt

super responsibility

inadequacy

confusion   anger

all together

special

develops independent life away from the family

**FAMILY HERO
SCHOOL JOCK
COMPANY MAN
SOCIAL NICE GUY/GAL**

FIGURE B

Family Scapegoat:

Primary function is to divert attention away from the dysfunctional person by inappropriate behavior. Internal emotions are extremely negative.

SCAPEGOAT

wall of defenses

wrong peer values

chemical use

feelings

loneliness   anger

withdrawal

fear   hurt

sullenness

unplanned pregnancy

rejection

acting out

defiance

FAMILY SCAPEGOAT
SCHOOL PROBLEM
COMPANY TROUBLE-MAKER
SOCIAL JERK

FIGURE C

Lost Child:

Primary goal is to escape by emotional and physical separation. Family does not have to concern itself with this child.

THE LOST CHILD

wall of defenses

withdrawal · quietness

feelings

loneliness · hurt

aloofness · distance

inadequacy

anger

sometimes overweight · being super-independent

rejection

**FAMILY LOST CHILD
SCHOOL DAY-DREAMER
COMPANY DRONE
SOCIAL LONER**

FIGURE D

Family Mascot:

Primary responsibility is to divert attention away from the dysfunctional family member by humor. The mascot feels unloved and worthless.

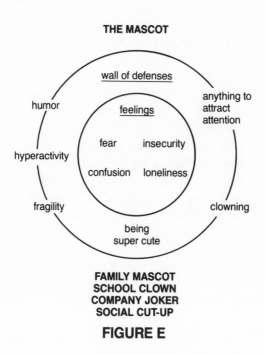

FIGURE E

As we look at these "survival roles," we begin to appreciate how they define the parts each member in the dysfunctional family will play. Interestingly, members may play several roles during the family's lifetime. And as the name implies, these roles are used as a means of surviving the family's traumas. One family I saw for nearly a year portrayed each of these parts so well.

David's And Donna's Story

David and Donna had a very stormy marriage. For most of its 14 years, Donna had clung to her marriage vows implicitly, especially the ones "for better or for worse." It was clear, early in their relationship, how David's abusive family background was significantly affecting him. As a boy he had experienced his father's rage and violence, not only against him and his brothers. He would routinely come between his father's blows and his mother. Now he raged and acted violent in his marriage with the least amount of provocation.

The grass hadn't been cut . . . Not enough money to pay bills . . . Traffic was bad coming home . . . were all reason enough to send him into a rage. His loss of self-control had also caused him many problems at work and with friends. Many a night at home their four children saw David screaming, throwing things and most unfortunately, physically abusing Donna.

Her family of origin had prepared her well for this marriage. Her father was an alcoholic who would regularly beat her mother and the children and then go off for days, abandoning them all. Her rationalizations for remaining in her marriage with David were: He wasn't an alcoholic, in fact, he rarely drank; he never beat the children; and after his rampages, he would sit and cry, asking for her forgiveness.

She had barely finished high school and never worked outside of caring for her home and children. Donna's fears of how she would survive financially, and her intense aversion to abandonment, which in her mind surfaced every time she thought of leaving David, kept her in this dysfunctional marriage. She played the "chief enabler" and protected David from all. When her friends confronted her about his behavior, she responded by saying, "He really didn't mean it," or "He's just having a stressful time at work." She sheltered him from as many consequences of his behavior as she could in an attempt to keep the family together.

Dawn, who was 12, had experienced this craziness the longest. She was the "family hero," and for her, early in life, she discovered that she had to be the family's self-image. She was an honor student, student council president, swim team captain and rarely was seen in public without her smile. Yet at home Dawn found little to smile about and her successes and accomplishments were seldom noticed amidst the chaos.

Billy was the "family scapegoat." At 10, he had already learned that he would never satisfy Dad. His acting-out behavior caused him problems in school, church and even with the police. David had made it known on more than one occasion that Billy was the cause of "this damn family's problems."

Michelle, 8, kept herself isolated and away from the action. She told me about this magical family she would visit to escape the yelling. It was interesting that David and Donna noted she was never a problem. "In fact," they said, "we hardly know she's there." Michelle had become the "lost child."

Finally, there was Mary, a laughing, happy seven-year-old. I asked myself on many occasions where she came from in this family of gloom. But Mary was the "family mascot." Since birth, she had made everyone laugh and smile, even in some of the most intense times. Mary could get David out of his anger often by mimicking his behavior. He told me, "I just can't be upset with her, she's so cute."

As we look at the roles played out in dysfunctional families, we begin to understand the immense power our family of origin has on our feelings, thinking and behavior. Families develop a dynamic or personality which sets the pace for most interaction between its members.

Laboratory Experiments

1. On this page, write down who your primary caregivers were. Now identify the secondary members. Draw a line to connect whom they affected the most in your primary family of origin. Next to the connection line, write what specific effects they had. As an example, my grandfather was a secondary family of origin member who impacted on my father. His posture set the stage for our family's basic mistrust of everyone.

2. On this page, write the Multigenerational Effects and list as many family traits, attitudes and beliefs as you can.

3. Using the members of your primary family of origin, identify who played the roles outlined by Virginia Satir. List each role and name the person who fit the role. Note: More than one role may have been played by the same person.

Three

Family
Personalities

Personality: *noun,* 1. the personal or individual quality that makes one person be different or act differently from another. 2. qualities of a person. 3. person or personage.

As a concept, personality has generally been regarded as a way to explain how people differ from one another. Their thoughts and behaviors are controlled by their personalities and direct the path they follow. Psychologists have studied personality for some time and the result has been the development of personality theories. Looking at an individual's personality has been the basis for most psychotherapeutic approaches in treating emotional-based distress. Psychoanalytic, cognitive, insight-oriented, reality and behavioral therapies have used personality dynamics to identify, understand and treat people.

27

Debate has persisted for some time around the issues of whether personalities are the result of one's environment and experiences or part of genetically inherited characteristics. This has been labeled the "nature versus nurture" controversy. Studies have supported both theories as explaining the development of our personalities. Although disagreement exists, there is support among professionals that personality dynamics function to control the individuals' thinking, behaviors and actions which maintain their despair, unhappiness and misery.

In working with adult children, it appears that their families have specific personalities too. The family's personality acts in the same manner as that of an individual. Just as personality characteristics define and model an individual's behavior, beliefs and attitudes, the family's personality affects its members by tempering their actions and reactions to one another.

Assessing the family's personality becomes an important process in unraveling the critical family of origin issues that fuel our own adult dysfunctions. The family secrets (don't talk, don't trust, don't feel) become personality characteristics of the family. Adult child families maintain these rules and all three are likely to be present as overt personality characteristics.

Families that operate using these rules contain many dynamics. They manifest themselves as families who are emotionless, self-destructive, impulsive, self-centered and selfless. They provide fertile ground in which adult children flourish and grow. The family's personality may be so powerful that it overrides any one individual's personality characteristics and demands conformity. Let me present some examples from my clinical practice.

Adult Child Family Personalities

Self-Destructive or Borderline Family: This family is characterized by extreme impulsiveness and unpredictability. The family often rages and acts violently with lots of instability. These self-destructive acts are purposeful and occur at a conscious level.

Kathy's Self-Destructive Family

Kathy was a 31-year-old woman, married for seven years

with two children. She came to therapy with significant depression and feeling totally out of control. Over the years she'd seen several psychiatrists and therapists, always leaving just as they began getting close to the emotional issues she found too painful.

Since the age of 13, she had reported being bulimic and generally felt her life had been unhappy and miserable. Binging on food had become a way she found to medicate her painful emotional past. She described herself as impulsive and having intense anger, often characterized by temper tantrums. She constantly questioned her career choice as a nurse and described feeling unfulfilled in almost everything.

When she wasn't depressed, she would have extreme periods of irritability and anxiety. The most painful part for her was the chronic feeling of emptiness which she identified as always being present. There were many occasions when she performed self-destructive acts, such as carving checkerboard designs on her arms with a razor or burning her legs with cigarette butts. Her marriage was just as bizarre and she would cycle between extreme emotions of love and hate for her husband and the children.

Kathy had all the characteristics of a self-destructive personality (sometimes called Borderline). Her family of origin had many of the same attributes. Mother's alcoholism and suicide attempts presented the impulsiveness and unpredictability in the family. Father was raging and violent and often became physically abusive to Kathy, her sisters and mother. The family's emotional state was always unstable. There was never any sense of wholeness or closeness. The family's personality had become Kathy's and now, as an adult, she was continuing to remain stuck in her family of origin's personality of self-destruction, defeat and misery.

Melodramatic Family (Histrionic): This is a family with very dramatic and reactive behaviors. It appears to need excitement all the time and teaches its members to worry, act helpless, be demanding and constantly seek reassurance. There is real conflict as "asking for help" identifies this family's desperation . . . not something it wants made public.

Sally's Melodramatic Family

Sally was a 34-year-old woman married for 13 years with no children. She experienced two miscarriages before coming to therapy and suffered extreme emotional distress with each. Yet even the pain associated with the loss of her pregnancies rarely competed with the anxiety and fears she had come to manifest over the years.

This woman was an emotional basketcase. She had a myriad of real physical symptoms and was not just acting like a hypochondriac. She might see a medical problem being discussed on a television talk show and call me the next day asking if I thought she needed to consult with her physician about the possibility of her developing that problem. Her obsession with physical complaints resulted in her eating to obesity. In fact, she found food was the only thing which gave her any temporary relief from worry and her physical complaints.

Sally was an only child and both of her parents carried on in the same manner. She told me that for years her mother and father would worry about the most obscure things and physical problems were high on the list. Obesity was present in her parents and the daily message was, "Eat this . . . and you'll forget about your problem." The family was constantly looking for ways to stop its worrying, yet it created numerous dramatic situations to maintain the nervousness and worry.

As an adult, Sally had taken on the family's personality and was acting it out in her daily life. She would eat out of control, worrying obsessively about ridiculous things, imagine she was dying and stress her marriage to the point of emotional and sexual deprivation. She developed the same melodramatic personality (Histrionic) as her family.

Perfectionistic/Self-Centered Family (Narcissistic): This family prides itself on the fact that mistakes are unacceptable. The image it presents to the community is one of perfection and unparalleled excellence. Its demands from the members are relentless and never-ending. This family sets goals which are never attained and the members constantly feel defeated.

Cindy's Perfectionistic/Self-Centered Family

Cindy was a 36-year-old married woman who first started seeing me four years ago. At that time, she had been a flight attendant for 14 years. Overall she was bright, attractive, a high achiever and energetic. Yet the first time we met, she had emotionally collapsed. The relationship with her boyfriend and family were both abusive.

As a small girl, both she and her sister had been raised by a New England family of the "utmost of protocol and decorum." Expectations of perfectionism were commonplace, and publicly this family appeared pristine. The two girls were always dressed as if they were "appearing on stage." In her adolescence, Cindy was told whom to date, where to be seen and how to maintain the family image.

Cindy's mother presented the model for this family's personality. Her father, although less intense, was just as adamant and held himself out to her as the "ideal male model." Cindy commented how outwardly both parents presented the epitome of excellence. However, in the privacy of their home, it wasn't uncommon to hear her parents complain of their inadequacies.

This family's personality had impacted on Cindy for years and with all of her successes and accomplishments, she found herself feeling chronically worthless, inadequate and unhappy. To the outside world, she presented the picture of style, confidence and grace. On the inside, she manifested the personality characteristics of her family: insecurity, constant self-demanding and extreme fear of failure. The demands were so great, she developed a multitude of physical symptoms causing her absenteeism at work and placing her on an indefinite disability.

Emotionless/Pleasureless Family (Anhedonic): This family is without emotional expression and often looks mechanical. There is a true absence of affection, ability to be happy, have fun or experience common family pleasures.

Todd's Emotionless/Pleasureless Family

Todd was a 29-year-old man whose second wife recently walked out on him. He described their marriage as closed

and uncommunicative. During most of their two years together, he saw himself as extremely passive and unable to
"ever have fun." Their relationship contained little affection
and intimacy, even from the very beginning. Mostly he described, they rarely experienced common pleasures even
while having sex. Interestingly his first marriage had many
of the same characteristics.

Todd described his family as controlled, emotionless and
regulated. His father, a dairy farmer, was a German immigrant
who was extremely ritualistic and never expressed any feelings. His mother followed the pattern set by his dad and rarely
showed her emotions or affection to the children.

He reported, "I can't remember us ever doing anything fun,
and living on the farm required us to work endless hours. We
would come in from school and immediately begin our chores.
Even holidays were pleasureless, as Dad felt celebrating was an
extravagance and others might think we were bragging."

Todd had become enmeshed in the family's emotionally
restrictive personality and now was struggling again in an
interpersonal relationship without being able to talk, trust or
feel. His family's personality was ruling his adult life.

> **Selfless Family (Co-dependent):** This family is marked by its
> intense preoccupation with what others think and do. At times, it's
> obsessional in its attempt to please, satisfy and rescue everyone.
> Like the material Silly Putty, its shape is formed and changed by
> others. It appears to press itself against people and groups, only
> picking up identity in this manner, just as Silly Putty will imprint
> when applied to something. If nothing is available, it is selfless.

Carol's Selfless Family

Carol was a 31-year-old single woman who came to see me
because of depression. After some sessions, it appeared that
she needed medication to help with her extreme mood
swings. Her family physician addressed this need and she
seemed more stable. But deeper and more complicated issues
surfaced, and we began moving toward her real problem. She
described feeling as though she had never had any self-esteem

or self-concept. Moreover, unless she could please or satisfy someone, she felt empty inside.

She had been in several relationships with men that were very one-sided. That is, she described them as all-giving and little-receiving. Her role was always to please the men, but she found it impossible to ever ask for any of her needs to be met. In fact, when I quizzed her about her needs, she was hard pressed to name one.

Her childhood experiences included a raging father who regularly beat the children and her mother, and a grandfather who would sexually fondle her every time she visited. As a method of trying to minimize Dad's violent temper and behavior, she recalled everyone always trying to please him.

"If Dad was happy about the baseball team winning, we would all pretend we were too. If Dad came home from work yelling about his job, Mom would coach us to say the right things so Dad felt we supported him." Everybody's identity came from her father's mood and behaviors. "No one seemed to have any identity of their own except Dad," she said. However, even her father didn't have any self-identity.

Carol's family personality presented a model which defined self as something you get from others. Finding any sense of meaning only came from what others would tell you. Self-worth, identity and approval could only come from others in this family. This co-dependent system teaches empowerment of others and traps one into a lifelong system of dependency — dependency on others. For her, it was the underlying motivation which directed her toward "needy men" who were great victims. Lacking self-worth, having no identity and starving for acceptance, cemented her into one sick relationship after another.

As a sick family's personality exists, the members of that family become infected with many of the same characteristics. They then take these with them into their adult lives and find relationships, jobs or marriages impossible to maintain. In fact, the needs they want the most are so often the ones they never seem to attain. Not because of others, but due to their lack of self-identity and how to ask for what they want and need.

Laboratory Experiment

1. Looking at each Adult Child Family Personality, decide which one represents your family personality. Write out the traits of your family personality below. If your family had its own unique family traits and characteristics, be sure to identify those as well.

Four

Adult Children
And Co-dependency

The decade of the '80s will be remembered in the history books as the years we elected a Hollywood actor to the presidency, interest rates soared to 20 percent and the concept of "co-dependency" evolved. Although the term "co-dependency" was known in the alcohol recovery field for years as the person allied with the alcoholic, Melody Beattie's book *Co-dependent No More* made it a household word by the end of the decade.

At the same time, the Adult Children of Alcoholics (ACoA) movement had begun. As 1989 drew to a close, hundreds of thousands of people were attending ACoA meetings across the country, attempting to find familiarity with others who experienced similar traumatic childhoods. Within the confines of these meetings, people started feeling, sharing and grieving, letting the recovery process begin.

Adult children of alcoholics and people living with an alcoholic became the first groups associated with the co-dependency definition. As we know, many different definitions appeared, but most were aimed at describing how these groups of people behaved and thought. However, from the outset of this book, I have addressed the problem of "adult children" as one which goes beyond the alcoholic family schism. It's clear that an even greater number of people suffered the same oppressive, repressive and dysfunctional childhoods as those of alcoholic families and, too, became co-dependent in their lives. This brief chapter's purpose is to identify those co-dependent characteristics which apply to our broader adult child population.

I remember hearing Robert Ackerman saying at a conference on adult children of alcoholics, "I'm not going to list all the definitions of co-dependency, because I'd like to get home before Christmas." That was 1987. In September of 1989, many of the original writers in the field of adult children and co-dependency met and discussed a universal definition for the term *co-dependency:*

> *Co-dependency* is a pattern of painful dependencies on compulsive behaviors and on approval from others in an attempt to find safety, self-worth and identity. Recovery is possible.

From this latest of definitions, we can see how it applies to people who would have come from many other backgrounds besides the alcoholic family. Many adults came from dysfunctional families where they experienced developmental impairments as children. The severity, duration and intensity of the impairments defined how they impacted on their adulthoods. The ensuing adult child has an entire checklist of things to determine how co-dependent she is. They are presented below for your own assessment.

Co-dependency Checklist

1. Overdeveloped sense of responsibility for everything — feels responsible for everyone.
2. Rigid thinking, sees things in very "black and white" ways, has problems being abstract.
3. Can't express feelings and often doesn't even know what he is feeling.
4. Finds trusting others extremely difficult. Can't get close to anyone.
5. Feels nervous and anxious much of the time — especially when nothing is happening (free-floating anxiety).
6. Constantly seeks approval — even when received, doesn't accept it.
7. Poor self-image and poor self-esteem.
8. Blames others for her unhappiness.
9. Doesn't know how to set healthy limits or boundaries for himself — can't say no.
10. Tremendous fears of abandonment — will do anything to avoid these feelings.
11. Feels victimized often.
12. Is always waiting for the other shoe to drop — anticipating the worst.

Amidst all the characteristics of co-dependency, it remains certain that the primary issues of co-dependency are childhood issues. Children learn how to behave and think in co-dependent ways as a reaction to the family's dysfunction. Being obsessive, controlling, rescuing and manipulative are the ways these children react to their sick families. These behaviors and thoughts then impact on the adult as they enter and begin navigating themselves through life. The main point is that regardless of your childhood, if the family had dysfunction, more than likely the children learned to behave and think in a co-dependent manner, further supporting the idea that adult children exist in far greater numbers than we ever imagined. Adult children of dysfunctional families struggle with the same emotional, interpersonal, insight and spiritual problems as their alcoholic family counterparts.

Laboratory Experiments

1. Go back to the Co-dependent Checklist. For each of the 12 items, rate the level of your present identification to the item. Use a scale of zero to four, with zero being "not present" and four being "present all the time." Total the score and use the scale below to determine your Co-dependency Index.

Index Range 0 — 12
Occasionally affected by others, but not generally a problem.

Index Range 13 — 24
Your level of sensitivity to others and the denial of your own needs is at a borderline stage. Certainly a lower score on this Index range indicates less severity, however, as your Index nears 24, your behaviors and dependencies on others appear co-dependent.

Index Range 25 — 36
An Index score in this range identifies many of your behaviors as co-dependent. Of greatest concern is the level of approval you seek from others to find any self-satisfaction.

Index Range 37 +
Serious co-dependent characteristics. As an adult child, your self-satisfaction and unhappiness are not going to change without a recovery plan.

2. Now identify the parent you think was most like you. Complete the Co-dependency Index for them and compare your scores with theirs.

Five

Sick Rules,
Sick Roles,
Sick Families

> **Rules:** *adverb,* 1. those things which others give us to
> follow; may be spoken, written or implied. Written ones
> are easiest to follow; implied rules require a course in
> mind-reading.
> **Roles:** *noun,* 1. a part as in a play which we are either
> expected to play or take on and master. Often we get
> cast into these by others to maintain their own needs.

Interestingly enough, the rules and roles people react to in
families so often are those which have been around for
generations. Our dysfunctional families are especially good at
maintaining those rules which perpetuate the family's sickness. The family secrets (don't talk, don't trust, don't feel) are
really rules the family uses as a way to protect and control
itself, to prevent outside influences from interfering in its

business. It creates the roles to ensure that the rules are followed. Let's begin by examining the rules and roles dysfunctional families develop.

Families: Rules: Roles:

We have already seen how dysfunctional families take on personalities. These personalities frequently dictate the rules for the family. This explains how the family's sickness operates and continues. A dysfunctional system requires dysfunctional rules to function. Likewise, if the family runs by "sick" rules, it will create roles for its members to act out that also support the sick system.

As an example, if the family says "Rules number one, two and three are we don't talk, trust or feel in this family," one parent will act as an enforcer to explain and punish those who don't comply. At the same time, someone will become the supporter or enabler in an attempt to keep peace and not rock the boat. As children we played many different roles in this kind of family:

Hero — Our job was to perform outstandingly and make this sick family look good in school, church, social occasions and the community at large.

Mascot — Our job was to make the family laugh and forget about its problems and difficulties.

Scapegoat — Our job was to become the target for the family, so they could blame someone for all of its troubles.

Caretaker — Our job was to take care of everyone. This included family, friends, pets, etc.

Mediator — Our job was to figure out everything and fix what seemed to be broken.

At times we may have played all of these roles yet the primary purpose for them was to provide a diversion from the family's real problems. The rules and roles of our families defined the boundaries that we learned to function within and sometimes attempted to escape. From these experiences we see how the development of boundaries sets the stage for our lifelong problems.

Developing Boundaries

Knowing what is acceptable, where not to cross the line and when something will be a problem are all issues that get defined by boundaries. Our families establish boundaries as a means to create operating ranges for all of their functions. In dysfunctional families the boundaries are dysfunctional. Even more problematic, they are ever-changing. Imagine what it would be like training for a particular job, only to find that before you reported to work, all the tasks had changed. Or if every few weeks the color of the stop lights were changed.

When sick families set boundaries, establish rules and cast members in roles, we have the makings of a good horror movie. The confusion and contradictions experienced by the children send them into adulthood with distorted ideas, beliefs and attitudes about life.

For a long time we've known that children can and do take on the dysfunctional characteristics of their parents. This was called *"folie au deux"* or "the illness of two." As the child bonds to a parent, that parent's behaviors and attitudes often become those of the child. This is enmeshment. Enmeshment is an ongoing process, which is important in understanding how the family's dysfunction continues with the children.

Most enmeshment occurs with the covert or unobserved behaviors we are exposed to. The child may see a perfectionistic and demanding parent who appears confident and self-assured. This parent's facade keeps their real feelings hidden. The child, unable to satisfy the demands of his parent, feels rejected, inadequate and insecure. Although not overtly shown, these are the parent's feelings as well. The child takes on the parent's covert feelings and the enmeshment process results. Remember the musical story of *Gypsy*? The mother suffered from the classic "stage mother" syndrome. If her daughter didn't achieve world fame and recognition, she would have failed in her role as a mother. But, as the story goes, Gypsy constantly complained of feeling inadequate and never meeting Mother's expectations. She went on to become an extremely successful performer, although she never felt accomplished.

The Teenager's Story

A real version of how this enmeshment works involved a 17-year-old boy who came to my office with significant concerns about his sexuality. In fact, he had become convinced that he might be gay. He based this on three specific events. First, he had only been on one date during his entire high school experience. Secondly, up until three months earlier, he had masturbated for the past two years. Finally, he found himself looking at other boys and admiring their looks.

As I explored his family of origin with him, we talked about his mother's and father's terrible marriage and divorce. There wasn't any affection or romance that he could recall. Father had been caught having multiple affairs, and at one point was even involved in a sex group involving men and women. This boy had never had any defined boundaries regarding what "normal" male and female relations were like. The sexual messages were extremely confusing and set confusing limits for him to follow.

The family secrets were in place and he found himself unable to talk about this to anyone. Trusting was out of the question and he had no idea what to do with his feelings. His father constantly belittled him and was rarely pleased with any of his accomplishments. This tragic boy thought he had become the failure his father had always accused him of being, and now he felt he had experienced the ultimate loss — the loss of his manhood.

The story has a happy ending. I showed him where he had become enmeshed in his father's self-concept. Then we cleared out the myths he had about sexuality and began defining healthy boundaries for his own sexuality. As his self-confidence began surfacing, he was willing to take risks and start socializing with girls. He took to dating like a duck to water.

What's important here is the idea that if we have a problem that doesn't appear to fit for us, it probably isn't ours. If it is someone else's problem that we have just taken on, we will never fix it, but continue to be frustrated by our inability to stop it. Once we become aware, we can begin to determine what we get out of maintaining it in our lives. Only then will we be able to advocate for ourselves and stop the enmeshment developing our own healthy boundaries.

Co-dependency And Our Families

Probably the strangest phenomenon I ever observed with family members in alcoholic families was how they had developed and taken on many of the same characteristics as the alcoholic. Their obsession with trying to control the alcoholic resulted in their behaving and thinking *just like* the alcoholic. The alcoholic was in denial and family members would minimize the problem as well. Especially those who feared that, if the alcoholic were confronted, he or she might leave. That was seen as worse than living with the alcoholism.

Another shared feature was the repression of feelings. Generally, besides rage and anger, the alcoholic never dealt with feelings. The family learned early on that to keep peace, you kept your feelings to yourself and remained silent. (Funny, I think we've talked about these little secrets before.)

Switching to other dysfunctional family types, I saw the same thing. The only difference was sometimes the severity was reduced. Yet as the family's dysfunction emerged, each of its members became obsessed with control issues and attempted to please or change the dysfunctional family member. The family's problem taught its members to be co-dependent. The co-dependency solidified the rules and roles for the family and in many cases defined the boundaries. Most obviously, it defined the family's dysfunction and acted as an agent for its continuation.

Laboratory Experiments

1. All families have rules to live by. Some rules are very well known and others are assumed or secretive. Take each example below and write out what rules your family defined.

    a. Rules about showing love, affection and emotion
    b. Rules about family secrets
    c. Rules about sex and nudity
    d. Rules about sickness
    e. Rules about jobs, work, family tasks
    f. Rules about food and eating
    g. Rules about drugs and alcohol
    h. Rules about religion
    i. Rules about safety and survival
    j. Rules about having a good time

2. Mark an M next to those that were Mother's rules, an F next to those that were Father's, and a B next to the ones that both held. Total the Ms, Fs and Bs.
3. Now list those rules you adhere to today. How many are Mother's, Father's or both?

a. _____

b. _____

c. _____

d. _____

e. _____

f. _____

g. _____

h. _____

i. _____

j. _____

_____

_____

_____

Six

My Family Tree

Family tree: *noun,* 1. a device which depicts the history of a particular family graphically. It has the capability to look across and back through generations to identify many specific family characteristics.

In the first interview with my clients, we start out by identifying some very specific family of origin information. The purpose is to explore and see if the problem they are presenting has any historical precedent. Medical examinations always include family history data as a routine part of the exam, especially when the physician is seeing a patient for the first time. Therapists as well need to ask and determine as much about the person's family history as possible. Adult children must be able to identify as many features about their families as they can. This process will help immeasurably in planning the course of treatment.

So often clients come to therapy wanting to "move on" from some emotional problem or situation and cannot understand why the obvious solutions won't work for them. As we talk, it becomes clear that they've continued to hold on to many emotional issues, preventing change. The fundamental problem exists because people rarely understand why their discomfort is present and, much of the time, it's masked by denial and self-delusion. Adult children have vast experiences with these concepts since their families used them to disavow what was really taking place. If any meaningful progress is to happen, we need very detailed pictures of their family of origin. That's why I begin therapy by having my clients prepare family trees. These trees give us a clear graphic representation of how, what and when things took place in their families. It shows the relationships between generations and where dysfunctions originated. You can create your own family tree and use this vital information later in the book to move toward solutions for your own recovery.

Developing A Family Tree

One rather unique way to obtain a family tree would be to take your least favorite relative and plant them in your backyard. A more conventional technique, however, is to create one graphically. This is how we're going to approach this task.

Family trees are a way of pictorially identifying family history. Creating this family tree graphically allows us to see the relationships and connections among members of our family. Our family tree will depict marriages, divorces, drug and alcohol dependencies, physical and emotional problems, causes of death, social problems and influence levels.

You'll need a fairly large piece of plain paper. An assortment of colored markers helps make the individual characteristics stand out clearly.

Family Tree Symbols (diag.)

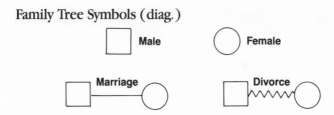

Begin by drawing your primary family of origin. Make sure you include brothers, sisters, step-brothers, step-sisters, parents and step-parents.

Diag.1

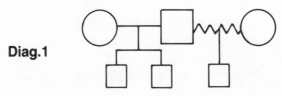

This diagram shows a man married twice, with boys from each marriage. (diag. 1)

Diag. 2

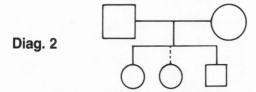

This shows a marriage with two natural children and one girl who was adopted (adopted = ----------). (diag. 2)

Use the following color scheme as indicated.

green	Alcohol/drug dependents are colored green.
⊙	Suspected alcohol/drug dependents are dotted green.
C	A red C indicates a person with cancer.
♡	A red heart indicates a person with heart problems.

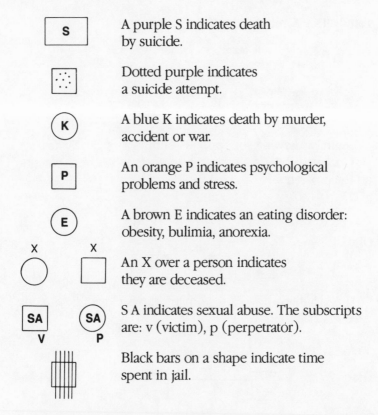

S
A purple S indicates death
by suicide.

Dotted purple indicates
a suicide attempt.

K
A blue K indicates death by murder,
accident or war.

P
An orange P indicates psychological
problems and stress.

E
A brown E indicates an eating disorder:
obesity, bulimia, anorexia.

X   X
An X over a person indicates
they are deceased.

SA   SA
V   P
S A indicates sexual abuse. The subscripts
are: v (victim), p (perpetrator).

Black bars on a shape indicate time
spent in jail.

Be sure to put first names by each shape. When your family tree is complete, it will present an excellent graphic representation of the characteristics which have affected you and others in the family. It shows the factors that have generationally been passed on to us. It gives us an instant picture of our family's history.

Draw Your Family Tree Here

Seven

Family Communication: Mythical Bonds, Beliefs And Relationships

Communication: *noun,* a sending, giving or exchanging of information or ideas. The ability to convey from one to another.

The process of communication, whether in business, school or socially, becomes a pivotal point as to how things become understood. Families likewise must communicate, so they too can function and carry out their business. The education, socialization, spiritualization and emotionalization of children in families are directed and controlled by the level of family communication.

Before we can begin recovery, the role our dysfunctional family's communication system played in our development must be understood. Our families are an endless resource for our understanding of how to live in the world. This chapter gives us the final pieces needed to begin applying what we've learned to the solutions of recovery. We finally will be able to "come home to ourselves."

Verbal And Nonverbal Communication

When things in families are dysfunctional, everyone in that family reacts to it. The communication system gives mixed, confusing and absent messages. These direct the actions and behaviors of everyone. Since 80 percent of family communication is nonverbal, members spend an inordinate amount of time trying to figure out what's not said or what's left out. We also attempt to determine what the feelings are behind these nonverbal messages.

In my own family, the message my grandfather overtly communicated was "You better get the other guy first before he gets you." This was especially true in his business dealings. However, the real covert message was "Don't trust" — our family secret. This got communicated through the family to my father and then to me. "Getting the other guy first" became a way to feel secure in the absence of trusting. This philosophy was acted out in their business for years. I observed it and even participated in this tradition, but never quite understood why.

I spent a lot of time attempting to determine what they were really feeling that caused this behavior. Their business was always good and they rarely had financial problems. So why were they so untrusting? The answer was to be found in our family of origin. The family's communication system kept it alive, generation after generation.

We learn from our family communication the rules and model behaviors to follow in life. Our families use communication to hide their problems and this allows dysfunctions to go on unaddressed. Whether the messages are verbal or nonverbal, the communication system in dysfunctional families sets up the family secrets to be protected and fuels our adult child development. Another important process in our development is called bonding. Bonding forms our attitudes and establishes behavior.

Bonding And The Mythical Bond

The process of bonding to a parent is just that: Attaching and likening ourselves to the parent we feel closest to. The parent we bond with tends to be the kind of person we seek out, as adults, to have relationships with.

As an example, Marcia spent the majority of her childhood being treated by her father like a princess. Throughout high school, she rarely dated the same person more than once, since princeliness was not characteristic of boys this age. After she finished college, she dated and discarded men regularly, finding that her standards were unattainable. She would either demand perfection from her dates or place them on a pedestal, becoming enslaved. At 36 she was still single, feeling desperate and lonely. Therapy provided a way to understand her family of origin's dysfunction, and help with changing the expectations she required in relationships. She had bonded with her father and, in spite of his chronic infidelity throughout his marriage, she made him the model male to look for in life.

Georgia was another woman who had lived with physical and emotional abuse throughout childhood. She had bonded with her mother who remained the victim, and Georgia found herself in one abusive marriage after another.

In many dysfunctional families, role reversal between parents and children occurs frequently. Rokelle Lerner, one of the founders of *Children Are People* (a program designed to help children in chemically dependent families), had two wonderful terms for this condition. When children take on their parent's role and responsibilities, this is called the "parentification of a child." When parents depend on and turn to their children for help with their emotional distresses, this is called the "childification of a parent."

We see this happen in addictive families, divorced families and families suffering from emotional and physical abuses. It commonly occurs when significant trauma strikes the family and outside assistance is not available. If we get bonded to a parent in this role reversal system, the greatest tragedy happens.

We develop what I call a "mythical bond." Becoming bonded to a parent who uses us as their support creates the following myth for us: "Our parent was there for us when we needed help as a child."

When children parent their parents, they must constantly deny the loneliness and pain of their childhood, due to the absent parent. In this case, the mythical bond results in our recreating this type of relationship with others, especially as adults. The kind of mythical relationships that ensue we describe as "It's really not that bad" or "She's really better than she seems."

Lauren had lived with her father since she was seven. Her mother had abandoned the family and never made contact again. For years Lauren had played the role of wife and mother to her dependent father. She said he rarely satisfied her emotional needs. After graduating from high school she married a man who also abused her. Her friends would plead with her to leave, yet she would reply, "He's really getting better."

She came to me after her 11th admission to the emergency room, where her head had been sewn back together. The mythical belief from childhood continued into her adulthood and was now threatening to end her life. She struggled with denial for months. Only after much reality confrontation did she decide to leave the abusive yet familiar-feeling marriage.

The family's communication sets up the rules to play by in our life. Our attachment to dysfunctional parents and the demands they put on us, nurture our adult child characteristics. Family secrets get established and transmitted, which perpetuate the misery. It's time to take this information and begin developing solutions for our recovery.

Laboratory Experiments

1. As discussed in this chapter, our families gave us messages which were never spoken (nonverbal), yet we understood them in many cases. In our dysfunctional families, we spent a great deal of time in identifying the "what wasn't said but meant" messages. Write below the nonverbal messages your family gave you and then the verbal ones.

_____

_____

_____

_____

_____

_____

_____

_____

_____

_____

_____

_____

_____

_____

_____

2. Identify which parent you bonded with. Describe how this parent generally treated you as a child. Now, as an adult, see if you can identify what impact that childhood bonding had on the kind of interpersonal relationships you enter into today.

_____

_____

_____

_____

_____

_____

_____

_____

3. In exercise two above, you're looking for information about bonding and a relational comparison between those experiences and your adult relationships you choose. See if you can identify what mythical beliefs might have existed for you and how you continue as an adult to look for those mythical beliefs in your present life.

_____

_____

_____

_____

_____

_____

_____

_____

Eight

Bringing It All Together: Beginning Our Recovery

> Recovery: *noun,* 1. the act or instance of recovering. A returning to normal health or prosperity; the regaining of one's balance or control.

The first seven chapters have concentrated on looking at the components that make up our family. Bringing together the information we've gathered will be this chapter's focus in formulating a plan for our recovery. This beginning will help us onto a "healthy path and the establishment of balance and control" in our lives.

We started out by comparing the similarities between alcoholic families and those with other kinds of trauma: divorce, separation, mental or physical abuses, etc. As pointed out, the same family secrets (don't talk, don't trust, don't feel) existed in both alcoholic and other dysfunctional families. The conclusion was "Dysfunction is dysfunction," "Sickness is sickness," and although the specific traumas of the families may have differed, there were common bonds among children of trauma in the sharing of developmental impairments.

We then looked at the multigenerational effects of these traumas on our families. Understanding what took place in our family of origin becomes significant in realizing and connecting how we began forming attitudes, behaviors and beliefs. As they developed, we began seeing the emergence of a family personality. Our adult child family personality fueled the family of origin's dysfunction and defined what impairments became the precipitants of our adult child characteristics. These may have included: poor self-image; feelings of inadequacy, obsessiveness, fears of abandonment, worry, and unhappiness. Next, we examined our adult child co-dependency.

Working through the Co-dependency Checklist gave us a level of our present Co-dependency Index (behaviors and thoughts). It also showed what impact our family of origin had on our index level. This data is needed in planning ways to stop our co-dependent behavior.

Our family tree presents an excellent pictorial review of the history in our family. The symbols show us relationships, mental and physical problems, dependencies, influences and social characteristics, all of which came to affect not only us, but everyone else in the family. This family tree information will be used for our family of origin inventory.

Finally, we identified the sick rules and roles our families developed, nurtured and operated from. The Rules Assessment helped us identify the boundaries and limits set by our family which, as adult children, we have held on to. These have prevented us from breaking away and learning how to establish healthy boundaries. We identified the family's communication style and learned to differentiate between what was said and what was not said in our families. This showed, maybe for the first time, what dysfunctions we became enmeshed in from the covert family messages. Now, we are going to organize the information we've gathered, to develop our own individualized recovery plan.

Individualized Recovery Plan

When adult children step up to the entrance of recovery, they come with many issues, experiences and problems. We've discussed the problems of adult children from alcoholic families and those from other dysfunctional homes. The two main deficits all these people have are their inability to identify and process feelings and the distortions in reality that enslave them. Both maintain their adult child characteristics. As you answer the questions below, note how many feelings get identified and realities redefined.

Use a separate sheet of paper to start your plan. In the left-hand margin, leave room to write out the feelings you experience while answering the questions. Also use this section to write out the realities you thought were present, but now realize were very different (old reality versus new reality — see Table 8.1.).

Table 8.1. My Recovery Plan

		Behaviors
Feelings:		
Anger, scared, sad	1. **Caretaker**	made excuses
Realities:	Mother	denied abuse
False Reality: Mom was stuck — couldn't leave		always unhappy
True Reality: Mom could have gotten help and made changes		

My Recovery Plan

1. Fill in who played these roles in your family and their behaviors

Rescuer-Caretaker

_____ B
E
_____ H
A
_____ V
I
_____ O
R
_____ S

Victim

_____ B
E
_____ H
A
_____ V
I
_____ O
R
_____ S

2. In the above diagram put a star by those behaviors you exhibit today.

3. So often as children we were recruited to play the role of an adult because our parent was dysfunctional. List those adult roles you played and circle the ones you still find yourself in today.

_____   _____

_____   _____

4. Identify your primary role as a child: hero, mascot, scapegoat, etc.

5. Answer the following:

"The way I feel about myself is most similar to _____." (which parent)

"This parent generally played the role of _____." (enabler, rescuer, dysfunctional, etc.)

6. List your family traits: examples are controlling, cynical, passive-aggressive, etc.

Put a star by the ones that you see in yourself.

1. _____

2. _____

3. _____

4. _____

5. _____

   7. Write your Co-dependency Index _____
     Write your mother's Index _____
     Write your father's Index _____
   8. List three major rules of the family you still operate by today that seem dysfunctional.

1. _____

2. _____

3. _____

The first part of our recovery plan is to have a detailed information sketch to work with and draw upon. The data we've gathered thus far give us an excellent base to use in Stage One of our recovery — understanding and debriefing. As you go through the recovery stage levels in the next chapters, if you find gaps or parts missing in your data, refer back to the chapter cited for the exercises. Probe deeper to get the details you need.

This will ensure the development of *solutions* to your problems and not just symptomatic fixes.

Robert Ackerman once described the adult children's motto for recovery as "Survive now, heal later." He went on to say, "Much later, . . . maybe 10 or 15 years later . . . or how about recovery by mail order?" Well, your recovery is beginning *now!* With our new direction and pace, you can do it.

Nine

Stage One: Understanding, Debriefing And Grieving

Understanding: *noun,* 1. the ability to understand.
2. The act of one who understands. 3. The power to
form reasoned judgments.
Debriefing: *noun,* 1. practice of extracting information
about an experience from its participants.
Grieving: *noun,* 1. to cause great sorrow, mourn, past
and present.

In this first stage of recovery, we're looking for information
which will explain how and why we developed our adult
child characteristics. At times we may feel that we've discovered information that allows us to "blame" others for what
we've endured. Let me emphasize one point. The purpose of
understanding is only to permit us the clarity we need to
begin dismantling those ideas and beliefs that have maintained our adult child problems.

We can never change or repair anything correctly that we do not understand. Many of our adult problems are merely symptoms of our adult child impairments. Treating the symptoms and not the causes of those problems would only continue our difficulties. In fact, blaming others for our problems in most cases would simply continue the same dysfunctional approach to life we experienced as children. More importantly, we would never improve.

Understanding Our Pain

Stage One of our recovery from whatever adult child dysfunctions we have must come from the insight we gather about our past. We've spent a lot of time assembling information about our family of origin. Determining how the family secrets began and their impact on us helped us see how the family's atmosphere evolved and functioned. As the definition of understanding implies, we must be able to explain the whys and hows of our family's dysfunction.

In my first book, *Addicted To Misery: The Other Side Of Co-dependency,* I talked about people who could indicate they were in emotional pain, but were unable to identify specifically what hurt. Adult children are extremely inept at identifying and processing their feelings.

This developmental impairment frequently occurs in families where the don't talk and don't trust family secrets are in force. The parents themselves are unable to deal with their own feelings, so they certainly cannot teach their children. The don't trust family secret keeps the family from getting any help, since this would be seen as a weakness or vulnerability.

But we can't let our family dysfunctions continue to control our adult lives. If we are to grow, we must understand our pain (understanding), let go of those past liabilities (debriefing) and grieve the losses of our childhoods (grieving). Only then can we move on to the next stage of recovery.

Stuck Points

The information we've assembled can help us determine where our "stuck points" are, and then make the changes to move on. Let me give you an example.

Margret's Story

Margret, a 36-year-old divorced woman, called me late one night, sobbing and extremely melancholy. She was experiencing an intense sense of loss, all related to her ex-husband. Although she'd been divorced for three years, she continued to feel that she would be alone the rest of her life.

Margret's family of origin history included her parents' divorce and a nasty custody battle which forced her to live with her father. Three months after the divorce, her father walked out, forcing her to live with an aunt. For Margret, trust and security issues became paramount childhood concerns.

Later after 11 years of physical abuse in her marriage, she got the courage to divorce her husband, Ray. But her old abandonment issues and acceptance needs were still great. Whenever I asked her what she wanted, she'd reply, "I know this sounds crazy, but I just want to go back to Ray."

Margret found it impossible to move on with her life because she refused to let go of the marriage. Until this changed, her pain would continue.

The trauma of her childhood was now fueling her adult child problems. Denial kept her from seeing things as they really were (an abusive marriage). Instead she developed a survival mentality to excuse the abuse. Her childhood needs for security and acceptance (which were rarely met) became her adult child obsessions. These she would pursue at any cost.

It took many sessions with Margret to help her understand how her childhood impairments resulted in her adult child dysfunctions. In Stage One of her recovery, understanding was the key to the recovery plan. Margret's stuck point was in not understanding why loneliness was so painful and controlling her feelings. She hadn't linked any of the past with her present emotional pain. In this case, Margret's stuck point was a true sense of not understanding the causal connection between her traumatic childhood and adult dependencies. This was impeding her recovery. Only after developing a working understanding could she begin the process of moving on to emotional satisfaction. Identifying stuck points is critical if any meaningful progress toward recovery is to occur.

As I noted, it took many sessions for Margret to advance. Years of denial and delusion had done their job and improvement was slow. The most deliberate and emotional process for her was what I call "debriefing" the traumas of childhood.

Debriefing The Trauma

Understanding what actually occurred during our childhood is the first step in recovery. We need clear information about our past to see how it relates to our adult child ways. We accomplish this through our insight and cognitive levels of awareness. However, all the insight in the world is of little help in our recovery unless we're able to talk and share about what happened.

I call this "debriefing the trauma." The principle comes from something psychologists have known for years: You should take victims aside as soon as possible after their trauma and let them talk about and process their experiences. The result is a lessening of the primary effect the trauma has on them and an improved prognosis for a return to normal functioning. We've all heard about this technique with victims of plane crashes and natural disasters; hostages; and returning POWs. Even before these people are reunited with their loved ones, professionals intercede and debrief their traumatic experiences.

Adult children are victims as well. Victims of traumatic childhoods need to debrief what happened if recovery is to begin. The debriefing of our childhood traumas lets us take the information we've identified and linked to our adult child dysfunctions and begin reducing the level of its effect. To recover, we must lower the anxieties, fears and sick beliefs we've maintained for so many years and start looking at our problems realistically. So often our perception of how things are is not based in reality.

Journaling

The debriefing techniques are varied and, at times, painful. I have clients keep daily journals or diaries of feelings. We are a virtual warehouse of stored-up emotions that must begin escaping from our controlled inner selves. The family secret, don't feel, created the need for us to learn, as children, how to stuff or internalize our feelings, rarely letting them be exposed.

This is probably the most destructive family secret and developmental impairment we experienced. It's the one that forced us to begin the painful process of keeping those things inside, not allowing the natural process of debriefing our feelings to occur.

Clients often respond by saying, "I really don't know what I feel, but I'm so uncomfortable I can't stand it." I have them begin by using the following four feelings as a guideline to determine what they might be experiencing at any given time: *mad, glad, sad* or *scared.*

I tell them that they might struggle with any one of these or experience all of them at any given time. Journaling opens a window to their emotional system, allowing feelings to come out (debriefing) and providing a safe avenue for their arrival.

One final note about journaling: I have clients write their entries using their opposite writing hand. That is, if they're right-handed, they must write using their left hand. If they are left-handed, they use their right hand.

At first this seems ridiculous, but it accomplishes two things. Adult children characteristically are perfectionistic. I used to get journals that looked like printed manuscripts. I even had some done on word processors. Their excuse was they wanted me to be able to read it. I assured them the purpose of this exercise was not to be considerate of my literary skills, but to let their emotions come out. It was then I decided that opposite hand writing would end this "picture perfect" presentation. Secondly, and more importantly, oppo- site hand writing appears very "childlike," and by writing like a child, we symbolically see ourselves as children. Since the process of stuffing our feelings began there, a symbolic return helps us get in touch with that inner child who desperately needs healing.

Letter-Writing

Another powerful technique to help us debrief our trauma is letter-writing. Many of us have been abused and still carry the pain and anger. I have clients write letters to their offenders, read them in therapy and then we burn the document. This, too, symbolically allows us to let feelings come out and, without risking reprisals, let go of our emotions. Ellen's therapy was an excellent example of how debriefing works.

Ellen's Story

For 32 years Ellen internalized her fears, anger and hurt over the sexual abuse that occurred with her brother as a child. By the time she came to me, she had seen four previous therapists, and her insurance company had all but denied any further coverage. She had been typed "addicted to therapy" and unlikely to improve. Most of what her previous therapies included were identifying and connecting what had happened to her (insight and cognitive-oriented psychotherapy). Her insight and awareness processes were excellent. Yet, she was unable to stop the intense feelings of inadequacy, poor self-concept or depression. She had tried anti-depressant medication with no improvement.

She had begun attending ACoA meetings with a friend several years earlier and, although her parents were not alcoholic, the restimulation of her painful childhood memories resulted in a crippling depression. She was reacting to the trauma of her childhood now. (This is called post-traumatic stress disorder or PTSD.) The insight she had gained was not stopping her present distress.

I had her begin opposite-hand journaling and write a letter to her brother. This letter included her feelings and was not an exercise in blaming. After we burned the letter, she was told to let go of those feelings and begin taking responsibility for her own emotions today.

She was no longer to let the past control and dictate how she was in the present. She was also told to maintain her 12-Step meetings, and I suggested Ellen begin attending CoDA (Co-Dependents Anonymous). Within several weeks, much of her depression and lethargy lifted and we were able to work on the next stage in her recovery: self-forgiveness.

Debriefing our traumas is a cleansing process that must occur so we can progress and finally grieve the losses of our childhood.

Grieving Our Losses

Elisabeth Kubler-Ross in her book *On Death and Dying* talked about the emotional processes people experience dealing with grief. She identified five stages that we must pass through to complete the grieving process: denial, anger, bargaining, depression and acceptance. The person suffering from grief can only move on and feel better after he passes through the first four stages and progresses to acceptance.

As adult children, there are many losses that we endured and must grieve if we're to move on and feel better. These losses include the loss of friendships, loss of boundaries, loss of spirituality, loss of rituals, loss of safety and the most important loss of all, the loss of memories. Regularly when I work with adult children, they find it difficult to remember much of their childhood, yet there seems to be a hollowness or emptiness that encompasses that time of their lives. There is no way to recapture what we lost in our broken childhoods. But before we can find mentors, learn how to parent ourselves and take control of our lives, we must grieve our losses.

The grieving process is accomplished by two techniques. First, we must identify the actual losses that occurred and our feelings about the losses. Secondly, we have to share the feelings with others who've had similar experiences.

Therapy can provide an excellent place to work on identifying our losses and the feelings we have. A technique called incident writing is helpful. Here you write out what happened to you as a child and how you remember feeling about it then. Next you write out your feeling about it today. Attending self-help groups (Al-Anon, ACoA, CoDA, etc.) will provide the format for our sharing. We find others there with the same losses and traumas we experienced, lessening our pain.

Once the grieving process is completed, we're ready to learn how to detach from our painful pasts and adult child dysfunctions — making way for self-forgiveness.

Laboratory Experiments

1. Identify and write out what you think were your childhood traumas and what the result has been in your adulthood. Try to determine where you might be stuck and write out what must change in order for you to move on.

Stuck Points:

What do you need to do to move on: let go, forgive, accept, understand, go through the pain?

2. Look at the example in Debriefing the Trauma and determine which process you would be willing to try to debrief your trauma. Do it!

3. As we discussed, we must begin the grieving process. Begin your own incident writing, and develop as much information as you can.

_____

_____
_____
_____
_____
_____
_____
_____
_____
_____
_____
_____
_____
_____

Ten

Stage Two: Detaching And Self-Forgiveness

Detachment: *noun*, 1. to separate or remove. 2. the state of being sent away. 3. freedom from involvement. 4. uninfluenced by other people.
Forgiveness: *noun*, 1. to excuse, pardon or cancel.

The solutions for the second stage of recovery are going to come from our ability to learn detachment (the process of letting go) and reach self-forgiveness (the process of stopping self-blame). These are significant in addressing our adult child problems. In Stage One we saw how identifying our stuck points and debriefing the traumas work to begin explaining the basis of our adult child realities and distortions.

The accompanying exercises were designed to help us see how distorted our perceptions were and then identify new ways to approach them. Grieving the losses of our childhood and finally gaining acceptance of what happened allow us to now move on with the recovery process.

Stage Two takes us further into the feelings arena and moves us on to the steps of accepting self-forgiveness. In this chapter we must learn to identify when we are attached to someone's emotional potential and how to detach from that bond. Lastly, there must be self-forgiveness to learn how and why we've blamed ourselves for so many problems that were not our own. These things must be mastered as solutions to this stage of recovery.

Detachment — Learning To Unattach

The concept of detachment has been around for decades as an element in the Al-Anon 12-Step program. The person who lives with an alcoholic is shown how they became attached to this person and their dependency. If any emotional peace, let alone any other peace is to occur, the Al-Anon member is told that she must learn to detach herself from the person's sickness.

At first this is confusing as well as frightening. Remember, this person has been caught up in the dependent person's life for some time, maybe years. She has learned to adapt to the crazy, unpredictable, frightening and unsatisfying life situations. Anyway, how can one detach from a person's disease and not the person?

On the surface, it seems that doing this would require us to become cold, hostile and withdrawn. This just isn't the case. But in learning to detach we acquire the skills to release ourselves from the other person's control and problems. We're taught to become responsible for ourselves and begin accepting that we are "powerless" over others. This powerless concept is extremely difficult to accept.

Often the person who lives with an alcoholic deludes himself into believing that, if he acts or responds in some particular fashion, that will control or alter the alcoholic's behavior. This is the denial mechanism that weaves him into the delusion of being in control and, more than likely, has maintained his painful existence for so long. This "veil of control" is a myth that must be broken if the person is to be set free.

Adult children also must discover how to detach, not only from their painful pasts, but from their adult child characteristics which control their daily decisions. As discussed, adult children suffered from developmental impairments while growing up.

Unfortunately, so many of us were taught that we were responsible for our parents' problems, or at the very least were obligated to resolve them. As a result we became "people pleasers," constantly trying to remedy everyone's distress. In the process we ignored our own needs. In learning to detach, our first challenge will be keeping our hands off other people's responsibilities and needs and not trying to control them.

If we learn to detach there will be many rewards. First we can shed the guilt and shame that has been controlling our behaviors. As children we often were manipulated by our family with shame and guilt, making it difficult for us to know sincere requests from manipulations. Another reward is no longer worrying about others and events that haven't occurred, giving us a sense of peace. But most importantly, we can learn to detach from the part of ourselves that has held us hostage as an adult child. We'll learn to advocate for ourselves, that is, doing what we need to "care for" ourselves. We learn that "taking care of" is reserved for children and sick people, and mature relationships only require "caring for." When we stop taking care of the people in our lives and begin caring for them, our growth and recovery continues.

This feature alone makes the work of learning to detach invaluable. As an adult child our ability to advocate for ourselves frees us from the bonds of emotional ransom and starts the process of self-actualization. This is the process of finding ourselves — discovering who we really are.

There are many solutions which will help you learn how to detach. I've listed four below to start you on the way. Look carefully at each one and decide how to apply them in your daily life.

1. Learn to identify when others are pushing your emotional buttons. Then create solutions which, at the very least, will remove you from that situation.

   One hint here. Our families are excellent people to push our buttons. But there is a good reason for this — they installed most of them.

   Sometimes when we want recovery, we begin expecting everyone to improve with us. Bad news! This isn't the case. Many times when we get better our families don't. Sometimes they even get worse. Remember, our responsibility lies with us.

2. When things around you seem to be chaotic, and you start feeling out of control and needing to respond, take a break, go for a walk, get into the bath, plan a vacation, take a ride.

   Take yourself out of the chaos! Remember, you can't fix everyone else's problems.

3. Look at what is happening. I mean *really* happening, not just your old perceptions. Define what are the problems and what are just the same symptoms that have been playing out forever.

4. Figure out what you need to do to take care of yourself. Learning to advocate for ourselves means identifying what we want and need and determining how to obtain it.

Detaching allows us to move away from the mythical beliefs that have maintained our adult child problems. We need not only to detach from our childhood impairments, but also the adult child attitudes and behaviors which preserve our predicament. Only then will our recovery begin and thrive. In doing this, our new peace with reality permits us to learn self-forgiveness.

Learning Self-Forgiveness

This part gets simplified when we've redefined reality. When we see that our emotional pain stems from our dysfunctional childhoods and not our inadequacies, a great burden is lifted. Forgiveness only comes from acceptance of a new reality, which is making peace with what actually happened in our lives and not what we perceived it to be.

Learning self-forgiveness requires some parenting. As we noted earlier, when addressing our losses as a child, our parents' parenting was less than adequate. In many instances they were just exhibiting what they had learned in their dysfunctional families.

In our quest for recovery, learning self-forgiveness requires us to get suggestions and directions from many new, but positive sources. Sponsors and 12-Step self-help groups are excellent for networking and providing an exchange of ideas. Another plan is to obtain a daily affirmations book (there are many available at bookstores) and begin reading the entries each day.

In your feelings journal, be sure to write out at least one self-affirmation every day. Make an effort to discover something you feel good about yourself and include that in the daily writings. Remember, learning to dislike ourselves came from long-term exposure to negative self-statements. The only way to extinguish those notions is by substituting positive, self-forgiving, self-affirming announcements. With time, we'll come to enjoy and accept the positive attitudes, eventually preparing ourselves for the next stage on our journey in recovery.

ELEVEN

Stage Three:
Learning To Play,
Finding Our Inner Child

Play: *noun,* 1. to take part in games or a game, to enjoy, to have fun.

This stage of our recovery, as ridiculous as it may sound, will be one of the more difficult accomplishments for us to achieve. Learning how to play, have fun, relax and do things to enjoy ourselves is an unknown to most of us. The mystery of all this and its elusiveness must be solved. When I ask my "adult children" clients what they do to have fun, they respond by saying, "I don't have time for fun, I'm too busy," or "I never really learned to play and have fun — I get embarrassed doing those things." These are very common responses for us.

To change this, we need to begin looking back at our childhood experiences and identify the "play needs" that we missed. Next, we must learn to differentiate between our child dependency needs and our adult ones. Finally, in learning to play, getting "childness" into our lives and not becoming "childlike" becomes the goal. This will bring us to the concluding stage of our recovery: learning to talk, trust and feel — resolving the problems our family secrets have produced.

Identifying Our Childhood Needs

In the section *Grieving Our Childhood Losses,* we examined the many things left out, missed or forgotten. Certainly in dysfunctional families, our playtimes often were missing. So many factors contributed to this void:

• Having to grow up fast
• Taking on adult responsibilities
• Becoming our parents' emotional support system
• Most of our time was spent on surviving
• Little time for recreation
• Living as a hostage
• Not knowing what was acceptable play

These things, as well as whatever else occurred in our families, dictated the atmosphere for our playtime. The most resounding reasons our dysfunctional families interfered with our functioning as children and having the chance to play were the significant role reversals that existed (children acting like parents, parents acting like children), and the unpredictability of what was going to happen next.

Children's play differs with their age category. For example, young children (three to five) have play needs which focus on social and gross motor skills. Things like pretending, dress-up, clay modeling, ball catching, sharing, swinging and taking turns fulfill these needs for this age group. Imagine how much fun it might be, as an adult, playing dress-up or swinging in the park. Older children (6 to 10) have increased social needs, want abstract activities and develop fine motor skills.

Their play activities include building things, reading, sports, art projects and group games.

The family secrets of dysfunctional families affect the child's experiences with play and in turn will limit what kind of play that takes place. As an example, the "don't talk" and "don't trust" family secrets teach children to fear others, feel insecure and isolate themselves as a means of protection. This greatly inhibits their willingness to engage in social play activities. It's unlikely that a child from this kind of family is going to enter into many situations which require participation. So the purpose in identifying what childhood play needs got ignored is to help direct us, as adults, to overcome our fears and meet those needs.

Take a piece of paper and write out the kinds of play you remember as a child. It's important to jog your memory, especially regarding those things you fantasized about or wished for. In our efforts to begin learning how to play, we want to get in touch with our inner child.

Child Dependency Needs Versus Adult Dependency Needs

There is a striking difference between child dependency needs and adult dependency needs. Children's needs are never satisfied. How many times have we become frustrated with a child (or watched someone else in the same predicament) when shortly after we get the child something she wanted, we see the child turning her efforts toward acquiring something else. Regardless of what they receive, it never seems to satisfy their wants. This defines what child dependency needs are: *It doesn't matter what they get, it's never enough.*

On the other hand, adults must learn to be satisfied with what they receive. Their needs must be tempered by the realities of life and what is within their grasp. *Learning to accept what we have and be content* is what defines how adult dependency needs are met.

In learning to play as adult children, we must be cautious of childhood needs which can direct us toward trying to fulfill our child dependency needs. This is a great set-up to keep us defeated and never happy with anything we attempt.

We must be cognizant of this and, although many of our childhood needs were unmet, it's important to begin finding satisfaction with what is achievable.

Playing Like A Child

When adults decide to get into play activities like softball, tennis or running, it always astounds me how hard they work at playing. The first thing they do is go out and purchase the most professional gear they can. Runners buy $100 shoes, nylon running suits and turn what children do so simply into a professional event. I had a client who was so in debt from buying expensive tennis equipment she had considered filing bankruptcy. What happened to playing tennis with a $20 racket and good ol' Keds?

I like to have clients get into play with simple activities. Things like: drawing, game playing, swinging, field trips or show-and-tell. As adult children our tendency is to want to do things perfectly. We turn play into work. So I emphasize the need to select play activities that are "fail-proof." That is, those that won't be judged as a success or failure. In learning to play, the object is to do just that: have fun, enjoy ourselves, recreate. Here are some suggestions I make to initiate play:

1. Go to a toy store and buy that special toy you've always wanted.
2. Take a field trip: go to the zoo or a museum.
3. Sign up for dance lessons.
4. Visit an amusement park.
5. Go to a video arcade.
6. Start piano lessons.
7. Go to the park and play on the slide and swings.
8. Do anything that turns you on.

We work together to develop lists of play activities, then plan a schedule, and they agree to participate in at least one activity per week during therapy. At first glance, this might not sound like much improvement. However, most of us aren't familiar with playing and having fun. We learned to be serious, guarded with our self-control and uncomfortable in new situations.

Now we must learn to play, have fun, enjoy ourselves and (a very unfamiliar experience) relax. This is an experiential problem for us, one which requires behavioral changes. With time, the proper shaping of our new response set (learning to play) will reinforce and reward its continuation, making it a valuable part of our daily life.

In shedding our adult child handicaps, it's important to remember that our goals are to become a freer spirit, less obsessive, more trusting and at peace with ourselves. Learning to play brings that childness we so desperately miss. Finding childness is merely letting the child within us come out, being able to have fun, relax and just find joy in playing. It isn't necessary in our recovery for us to become children or "childlike."

We must discover the wonderment of our inner child and allow that to release whatever holds us in emotional servitude. Innocent children uncontaminated by adult restrictions have freedoms we desperately seek. Learning to play sets into motion one of these freedoms that allows our recovery.

TWELVE

Stage Four: Talk, Trust And Feel

Talk: *verb,* 1. to express ideas, thoughts, etc. 2. to convey ideas to someone, letting thoughts emerge.

Trust: *noun,* 1. confidence in a person or thing because of the qualities one perceives or seems to perceive in him or it.

Feel: *noun,* 1. to experience an emotion, to feel sympathy, to sense, to experience the effects of. 2. to affect one's senses as being.

This book's main goal has been two-fold. First, to identify a vastly greater number of people who experienced family dysfunction and developmental impairments beyond those of alcoholic families. Secondly, to show that these people from dysfunctional families were exposed to the same family secrets causing them a multitude of emotional problems. We call them the "new adult children."

This group of adults has been struggling with self-esteem, acceptance, interpersonal relationships, boundaries and a myriad of emotional issues, which constantly control and maintain their despair and frustrations. At the root of their displaced inner selves is the dysfunctional family of origin they traveled through. As in the alcoholic family, these families elected to regulate and manage their affairs by very devisive means. These means became sealed from the outside world, letting their dysfunctional conspiracies exist. These were their family secrets, not to be made public. At the core of most sick families, allowing their existence, are their rules: don't talk, don't trust and don't feel.

We've progressed through the pages outlined in the previous chapters. We're now at the stage where we can defy those repressive rules and take charge of our own direction. We can talk — about ourselves, our needs, our beliefs and our values. We can trust — not only others, but ourselves, to allow our judgments to be validated. And at last we can feel — feel the feelings we've locked away and tried to repress, only to ache inside in silent misery. We need to change our family secrets to broken family myths, and allow our celebration of talking, trusting and feeling to go forward.

Talk, Trust And Feel

Think about this today:

- To laugh is to risk appearing a fool.
- To weep is to risk appearing sentimental.
- To reach out for another is to risk involvement.
- To expose feelings is to risk exposing your true self.
- To place your ideas, your dreams, before the crowd is to risk their loss.
- To love is to risk not being loved in return.
- To live is to risk dying.
- To hope is to risk despair.
- To try is to risk failure.

But risks must be taken because the greatest hazard in life is to risk nothing. The person who risks nothing, does nothing, has nothing, is nothing. He may avoid suffering and sorrow, but he simply cannot learn, feel, change, grow, love or live. Chained by his certitudes, he is a slave, he has forfeited freedom. Only a person who risks is free.

The actual sources of these two passages are unknown, yet they appear in the texts of family treatment programs everywhere. For our purposes, they define everything we have worked on to this point. They emphasize the predominant issue behind our recovery — risk. Without our willingness to risk, we would never step out onto the stage of recovery.

At the heart of these messages is "We must take whatever risks are necessary so that we will no longer remain silent (don't talk), avoid taking chances (don't trust), and pretend not to feel (don't feel)." We must talk about our needs, find the courage to trust ourselves and recognize our feelings. Our talking, trusting and feeling allow us to practice new methods on old problems. Problems which have previously left us frustrated, worried and out of sorts.

Look at these examples of how we can deal with old problems:

1. Airing resentments: Our new personal rules give us permission to talk about those things that disturb us.
2. Letting go of the past: We find that processing our feelings removes the barriers that up to this point have maintained our adult child characteristics.
3. How to start over with honesty and openness: The freedom of trusting lets us be open with our needs and gives us a second chance.
4. How to risk: Being able to trust ourselves permits growth as we try out our new experiences.
5. How to communicate: Up until this point, talking was merely to correspond. In recovery, talking is less sharing, explaining and a tool we will use for making known our needs.
6. How to listen: For the first time we can hear what others say and let our guard down, realizing we're in control of ourselves.

Our Basic Solutions

As adult children, our recovery is predicated on some rather basic solutions. We must first understand what our real problems are. That is, discover why our self-esteem is low, why we enter and remain in unfulfilling interpersonal relationships, why we have intense feelings of shame and guilt with regard to our families, or whatever else acts to govern and effect the pain and frustrations in our lives. Understanding what keeps us paralyzed, when the solutions are so often clear to us, is vital if our recovery is to begin.

Our perceptions must become the realities that exist, as difficult as they may be to face. Real understanding must take place if we're going to discard our adult child constraints. This comes from being able to talk openly, honestly and freely about our pasts. Our learning to talk, not of things, but of ourselves, is the first solution needed for recovery.

The next solution in the maze of recovery is to reach out and look for new ways to tackle the problems we've had. Many of us have spent years trying to solve some interpersonal problems, only to stay frustrated and miserable. Friends, family and even strangers have made suggestions. We end up saying to ourselves, "If we only knew that would work" or "I wish I could take that risk."

At the core of our frustration is our basic inability to trust. Trust that others may know something that we don't or trust that, if the suggestion doesn't work, we can and will survive the outcome.

I used to say to patients in the chemical dependency units, "We don't want very much from you — we just want you to give up everything and do it quickly." Only in taking that ultimate leap of faith and trusting others will our recovery begin. Our recovery's second solution is formulated by our learning to trust, not in a blind manner, but by disregarding those archaic and often paranoid delusions our family of origin presented. We must exercise this skill in many situations and do it often.

To feel is divine. To feel is to release. To feel is to experience. Feeling becomes the third solution that frees us, like water flowing through the dam. When closed, the pressure builds and rage intensifies, creating a destructive backlash. Like the water, our feelings need a path to come out and dissipate their intensity. Feeling becomes the solution to end the emotional barriers and purify our soul and our being.

Altogether these solutions give us recovery. Interwoven with one another, they establish the ways and means to release us from being adult children and give us self, substance, respect, meaning and the true sense of being an "adult."

Recovery

Recovery is a wonderful experience. It's the process of learning to feel good about ourselves and finding healthy ways to get our needs met. It shows us ways to cope with stress and deal with our feelings. But the greatest result from recovery is discovering our own specialness, the part of ourselves that we've been searching for years.

Client after client I work with begins therapy by stating, "No matter what I do or accomplish, I never feel right with myself. It's as if I'm missing 'me.' Nothing about myself feels special or unique." This describes the missing spiritual self of adult children.

In recovery we break from this self-absence and discover a sense of meaning for ourselves. This happens as a result of understanding what has really happened to us, learning self-forgiveness, and finally extinguishing the family secrets from our lives.

At a recent conference on adult children, I heard Robert Ackerman, author of *Perfect Daughters,* talk about the wonderment of recovery. He pointed out that "our recovery is a process which continues on forever. By removing the *y* and adding *ing* to the word recovery, it becomes recovering, meaning to go as far as you can — never ending."

This message makes our "self" work so important and fulfilling. We can go as far as we want! We don't have to allow our childhood impairments or traumas to control today. Working through the process of understanding our "adult child" pains and frustrations reframes for us those early experiences, to pardon our responsibilities. Finally grieving the losses of our childhood lets us move on, discovering new ways to achieve those missing parts. The method of detachment teaches us how to give up those hurtful past memories. It also shows us how to stop that part of our adult self which has acted to sabotage and promote our problems. Recovering establishes the meanings, not only for ourselves, but our lives.

I came across the *ABC's Of Recovery* at a 12-Step meeting recently. Their simplicity is clear and suggestions appropriate. I encourage you to incorporate each letter into your own recovery. They offer alternatives to the way we function and allow our inner selves to grow. (See Fig. 1.)

ABC's Of Recovery
By Pat A. & Kit W.

Old		New
ALWAYS be afraid	—A—	ALWAYS try to identify and work through your fears
BECOME invisible - don't risk rejection	—B—	BECOME visible - discover and own your personal power
CRY alone in the dark	—C—	CRY without shame
DEVELOP heavy-duty defenses	—D—	DEVELOP appropriate boundaries
ESCAPE life in whatever way you can	—E—	EMBRACE life
FIGURE out what people want and try like hell to deliver	—F—	FIGURE out what you need and try to find ways to get it
GIVE until it hurts and then give some more	—G—	GIVE when you want to give and have enough
HIDE your feelings and hope they go away	—H—	HOLD onto your right to feel
IGNORE your instincts and intuitions	—I—	INVITE yourself to trust your gut
JUSTIFY and explain	—J—	JUST be true to yourself
KEEP hoping things will get better	—K—	KEEP working to make yourself feel better
LOSE your dreams	—L—	LET your dreams leap from your heart
MINIMIZE your losses and keep going	—M—	MOURN your losses and keep growing
NUMB out to get through	—N—	NOTICE when you numb out and ask yourself why
OBSESS about things you cannot change	—O—	ONLY try to change yourself
PRETEND it's not really so bad	—P—	PUT the lights on and admit the truth about your life
QUIT caring about yourself	—Q—	QUIT hurting yourself
RETREAT into your shell	—R—	REACH out for help
SURVIVE	—S—	SOAR
TRUST no one	—T—	TRUST when you feel safe
USE - drugs, alcohol, food, sex, people	—U—	USE your program & support network
VICTIM mentally	—V—	VICTORIOUS attitude
WHO cares? Why me? Where can I run?	—W—	WORK the steps
X-RAY eyes see through to every defect	—X—	X-PECT progress, not perfection
YEARS of buried pain and regret	—Y—	YEARS of self-discovery and promise
ZEALOUSLY guard yourself	—Z—	ZEALOUSLY care for yourself

We must move from the adult child bonds, controlled by our family secrets. At the time of her original work, it would have been hard to imagine what impact Claudia Black's family secrets (don't talk, don't trust, don't feel) would have on people besides adults from alcoholic families. So many others from dysfunctional families have struggled with problems in their lives as a result of the same family secrets.

There *is* a way out of the repressive corridors these secrets have maintained. Hopefully, this book has given you new solutions to old problems, allowing you to escape from the adult child schism.

One final comment. As adult children, we often expect perfection. Therefore, it wouldn't be surprising to feel that, once changes are made to stop our frustrations and misery, we should never be troubled by our adult child ways again. In fact, we might regard a return to any of the symptoms as a failure. But things won't be perfect. We'll always respond to our own human frailties. Our goal is to reduce the despair and unhappiness and begin enjoying life. But who said life was without pain or discomfort? What a bore it would be without some diversion. Anyhow, now we can work to *solve* our problems, instead of just surviving them.

Good Luck!

Suggested Reading

Ackerman, Robert J., **Children Of Alcoholics: A Guidebook For Educators, Therapists And Parents,** (2nd Ed.). Holmes Beach, FL: Learning Publications, 1983.

Ackerman, Robert J., **Let Go And Grow,** Pompano Beach, FL: Health Communications, 1987.

Beattie, Melody, **Co-dependent No More,** Center City, MN: Hazelden, 1987.

Becker, Robert A., **Addicted To Misery: The Other Side Of Co-dependency,** Deerfield Beach, FL: Health Communications, 1989.

Black, Claudia, **It Will Never Happen To Me,** Denver, CO: Medical Administration Company, 1982.

Cermak, Timmen L., **A Primer On Adult Children Of Alcoholics,** Deerfield Beach, FL: Health Communications, 1989.

Elkin, M., **Families Under The Influence: Changing Alcoholic Patterns,** New York: W. W. Norton, 1984.

Fishel, Ruth, **Time For Joy Daily Affirmations,** Deerfield Beach, FL: Health Communications, 1990.

Friel, John and Friel, Linda, **Being Functional: A No-Nonsense Guide To What's Normal,** Deerfield Beach, FL: Health Communications, 1990.

Kubler-Ross, E., **On Death And Dying,** New York: Macmillan, 1969.

Larsen, E., **Stage II Recovery: Life Beyond Addiction,** San Francisco, CA: Harper and Row, 1985.

Lee, John, **The Flying Boy: Healing The Wounded Man**, Deerfield Beach, FL: Health Communications, 1989.

Lerner, Rokelle, **Daily Affirmations: For Adult Children Of Alcoholics**, Pompano Beach, FL: Health Communications, 1985.

Middelton-Moz, Jane, **Children Of Trauma: Rediscovering Your Discarded Self**, Deerfield Beach, FL: Health Communications, 1989.

Middelton-Moz, Jane, **Shame And Guilt: Masters Of Disguise**, Deerfield Beach, FL: Health Communications, 1990.

Powell, John, **Why Am I Afraid To Tell You Who I Am?** Niles, IL: Argus Communications, 1969.

Steiner, C., **Scripts People Live**, New York: Grove Press, 1979.

Subby, Robert, **Healing The Family Within**, Deerfield Beach, FL: Health Communications, 1990.

The 12 Steps For Adult Children, San Diego, CA: Recovery Publications, 1987.

Twerski, Abraham J., **Addictive Thinking: Why Do We Lie To Ourselves? Why Do Others Believe Us?** City Center, MN: Hazelden, 1990.

Wegscheider, Sharon, **Another Chance: Hope And Health For Alcoholic Families**, Palo Alto, CA: Science and Behavior Books, 1980.

Whitfield, Charles L., **Healing The Child Within**, Pompano Beach, FL: Health Communications, 1987.

Wills-Brandon, Carla, **Learning To Say No: Establishing Healthy Boundaries**, Deerfield Beach, FL: Health Communications, 1990.

Woititz, J. G., **Adult Children Of Alcoholics**, Pompano Beach, FL: Health Communications, 1983.

Woititz, Janet G., and Garner, Alan, **Lifeskills For Adult Children**, Deerfield Beach, FL: Health Communications, 1990.

Bibliography

Ackerman, Robert J., **Children of Alcoholics: A Guidebook For Educators, Therapists And Parents,** (2nd Ed.). Holmes Beach, FL: Learning Publications, 1983.

Ackerman, Robert J., **Let Go And Grow,** Deerfield Beach, FL: Health Communications, Inc., 1987.

Alcoholics Anonymous, **Twelve Steps and Twelve Traditions,** A.A. World Services, New York, 1952.

Beattie, Melody, **Co-dependent No More,** Center City, MN: Hazelden, 1987.

Becker, Robert A., **Addicted To Misery: The Other Side of Co-dependency,** Deerfield Beach, FL: Health Communications, 1989.

Black, Claudia, **It Will Never Happen To Me,** Denver, CO: Medical Administration Company, 1982.

Cermak, Timmen L., **Diagnosing And Treating Co-dependency,** MN: Johnson Institute Books, 1986.

Cermak, Timmen, L., **A Primer On Adult Children Of Alcoholics,** Deerfield Beach, FL: Health Communications, 1989.

Cork, Margaret R., **The Forgotten Children,** Toronto: Addiction Research Foundation, 1969.

Dowling, Colette, **The Cinderella Complex — Women's Hidden Fears of Independence,** New York: Pocket Books, 1981.

Elkin, M., **Families Under The Influence: Changing Alcoholic Patterns,** New York: W. W. Norton, 1984.

Fishel, Ruth, **Time For Joy Daily Affirmations,** Deerfield Beach, FL: Health Communications, 1990.

Forward, Susan, **Toxic Parents**, New York: Bantam, 1986.

Friel, John and Friel, Linda, **Being Functional: A No-Nonsense Guide To What's Normal**, Deerfield Beach, FL: Health Communications, 1990.

Halpern, Howard, **How To Break Your Addiction To A Person**, New York: Bantam, 1983.

Kubler-Ross, E., **On Death And Dying**, New York: Macmillan Publishing Company, 1969.

Larsen, E., **Stage II Recovery: Life Beyond Addiction**, San Francisco, CA: Harper and Row, 1985.

Lee, John, **The Flying Boy: Healing The Wounded Man**, Deerfield Beach, FL: Health Communications, 1989.

Lerner, Rokelle, **Daily Affirmations: For Adult Children of Alcoholics**, Pompano Beach, FL: Health Communications, 1985.

Lerner, Rokelle, "Young Children of Alcoholics," lecture presented at Seventh Annual Fall Conference on Alcoholism, Virginia Beach, Virginia, October 28-30, 1987.

Middelton-Moz, Jane, **Children Of Trauma: Rediscovering Your Discarded Self**, Deerfield Beach, FL: Health Communications, 1989.

Middelton-Moz, Jane, **Shame And Guilt: Masters Of Disguise**, Deerfield Beach, FL: Health Communications, 1990.

Phelps, Janice K., and Nourse, Alan E., **The Hidden Addictions And How To Get Free**, Boston: Little Brown, 1986.

Powell, John, **Why Am I Afraid To Tell You Who I Am?**, Niles, IL: Argus Communications, 1969.

Rubin, Theodore, **The Angry Book**, New York: MacMillan, 1970.

Steiner, C., **Scripts People Live**, New York: Grove Press, 1979.

Subby, Robert, **Lost In The Shuffle: The Co-dependent Reality**, Pompano Beach, FL: Health Communications, 1987.

Subby, Robert, **Healing The Family Within**, Deerfield Beach, FL: Health Communications, 1990.

The 12 Steps For Adult Children, San Diego, CA: Recovery Publications, 1987.

Twerski, Abraham J., **Addictive Thinking: Why Do We Lie To Ourselves? Why Do Others Believe Us?**, City Center, MN: Hazelden, 1990.

Wegscheider, Sharon, **Another Chance: Hope And Health For The Alcoholic Family**, Palo Alto, CA: Science and Behavior Books, 1980.

Whitfield, Charles L., **Healing The Child Within**, Pompano Beach, FL: Health Communications, 1987.

Wills-Brandon, Carla, **Learning To Say No: Establishing Healthy Boundaries**, Deerfield Beach, FL: Health Communications, 1990.

Woititz, J. G., **Adult Children of Alcoholics**, Pompano Beach, FL: Health Communications, 1983.

Woititz, Janet G., and Garner, Alan, **Lifeskills For Adult Children**, Deerfield Beach, FL: Health Communications, 1990.

New Books...
from Health Communications

ALTERNATIVE PATHWAYS TO HEALING: The Recovery Medicine Wheel
Kip Coggins, MSW
This book with its unique approach to recovery explains the concept of the
medicine wheel — and how you can learn to live in harmony with yourself,
with others and with the earth.
ISBN 1-55874-089-9 $7.95

UNDERSTANDING CO-DEPENDENCY
Sharon Wegscheider-Cruse, M.A., and Joseph R. Cruse, M.D.
The authors give us a basic understanding of co-dependency that everyone
can use — what it is, how it happens, who is affected by it and what can
be done for them.
ISBN 1-55874-077-5 $7.95

THE OTHER SIDE OF THE FAMILY:
A Book For Recovery From Abuse, Incest And Neglect
Ellen Ratner, Ed.M.
This workbook addresses the issues of the survivor — self-esteem, feelings,
defenses, grieving, relationships and sexuality — and goes beyond to help
them through the healing process.
ISBN 1-55874-110-0 $13.95

OVERCOMING PERFECTIONISM:
The Key To A Balanced Recovery
Ann W. Smith, M.S.
This book offers practical hints, together with a few lighthearted ones, as a
guide toward learning to "live in the middle." It invites you to let go of your
superhuman syndrome and find a balanced recovery.
ISBN 1-55874-111-9 $8.95

LEARNING TO SAY NO:
Establishing Healthy Boundaries
Carla Wills-Brandon, M.A.
If you grew up in a dysfunctional family, establishing boundaries is a
difficult and risky decision. Where do you draw the line? Learn to recognize
yourself as an individual who has the power to say no.
ISBN 1-55874-087-2 $8.95

3201 S.W. 15th Street,
Deerfield Beach, FL 33442-8190
1-800-851-9100

Health
Communications, Inc.

Daily Affirmation Books from . . .
Health Communications

GENTLE REMINDERS FOR CO-DEPENDENTS: Daily Affirmations
Mitzi Chandler

With insight and humor, Mitzi Chandler takes the co-dependent and the adult child through the year. Gentle Reminders is for those in recovery who seek to enjoy the miracle each day brings.
ISBN 1-55874-020-1   **$6.95**

TIME FOR JOY: Daily Affirmations
Ruth Fishel

With quotations, thoughts and healing energizing affirmations these daily messages address the fears and imperfections of being human, guiding us through self-acceptance to a tangible peace and the place within where there is *time for joy.*
ISBN 0-932194-82-6   **$6.95**

AFFIRMATIONS FOR THE INNER CHILD
Rokelle Lerner

This book contains powerful messages and helpful suggestions aimed at adults who have unfinished childhood issues. By reading it daily we can end the cycle of suffering and move from pain into recovery.
ISBN 1-55874-045-6   **$6.95**

DAILY AFFIRMATIONS: For Adult Children of Alcoholics
Rokelle Lerner

Affirmations are a way to discover personal awareness, growth and spiritual potential, and self-regard. Reading this book gives us an opportunity to nurture ourselves, learn who we are and what we want to become.
ISBN 0-932194-47-3
(Little Red Book)   **$6.95**
(New Cover Edition)   **$6.95**

SOOTHING MOMENTS: Daily Meditations For Fast-Track Living
Bryan E. Robinson, Ph.D.

This is designed for those leading fast-paced and high-pressured lives who need time out each day to bring self-renewal, joy and serenity into their lives.
ISBN 1-55874-075-9   **$6.95**

3201 S.W. 15th Street,
Deerfield Beach, FL 33442-8190
1-800-851-9100

**Health
Communications, Inc.**